# BEYOND BLING

## Voices of Hip-Hop in Art

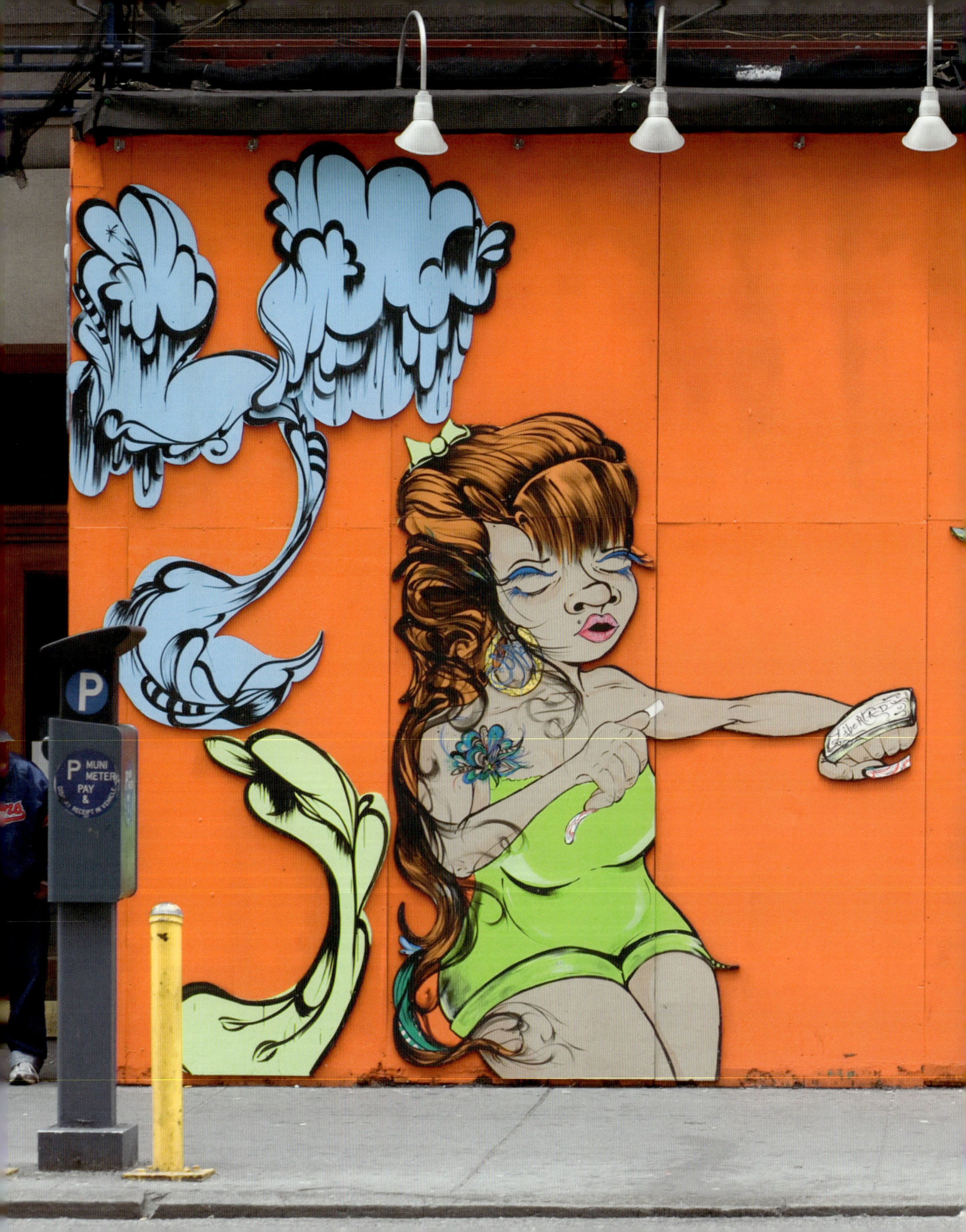
P
P MUNI METER
PAY
&

# BEYOND BLING

## Voices of Hip-Hop in Art

MATTHEW McLENDON

The John and Mable Ringling Museum of Art, The State Art Museum of Florida,
The Florida State University in association with Scala Publishers

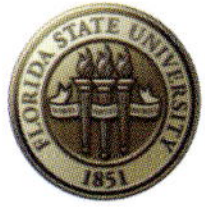

SCALA

# CONTENTS

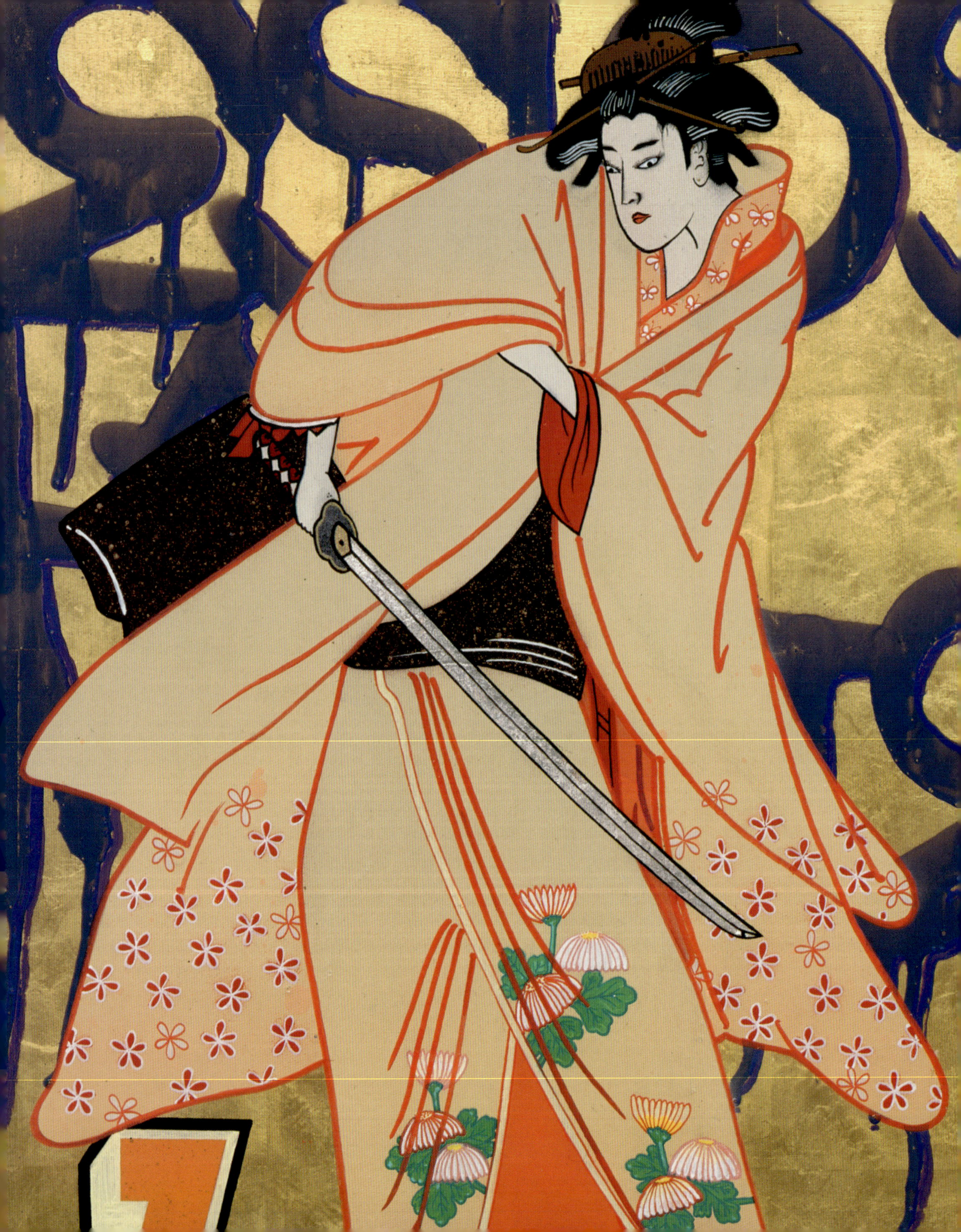

# FOREWORD

The John and Mable Ringling Museum of Art has long been acknowledged as one of the pre-eminent collections of Old Master paintings in America. Best known for its monumental *Triumph of the Eucharist* cartoons by the Flemish Baroque artist Peter Paul Rubens, what is perhaps less well known is that The Ringling has a long history of engagement with modern and contemporary art. Though John Ringling's collection interests really end with the late nineteenth century, the first director of the museum, A. Everett "Chick" Austin, was a pivotal figure in the reception of twentieth-century modernism in the United States. With his characteristic flair, Chick ensured that the museum would not only look to the past but to the present and future as well.

*Beyond Bling: Voices of Hip-Hop in Art* is the first exhibition at the Museum of Art to fall under the banner of the museum's new initiative, Art of Our Time. Art of Our Time encompasses visual and performance arts in both the galleries and the Historic Asolo Theater and demonstrates the museum's renewed commitment to the important dialogue between historic and contemporary artists. It is with great pleasure that I welcome the dynamic young artists who comprise the exhibition to the museum. I would also like to extend my appreciation to the galleries and collectors who have been so giving of their time and resources to bring this project to fruition.

Hip-hop culture has been on the ascendant since the late 1970s. While there have been notable shows within the last decade that have explored the history of hip-hop's influence in contemporary art, this exhibition is the first of its kind with a very tight focus on work produced in the first decade of this "new" millennium. These ten artists who have incorporated hip-hop/street culture into their oeuvre in provocative manners encourage us to question and expand our ideas of what it means to speak with a particularly urban voice in this time of advanced globalization and capitalism.

As always, an exhibition such as this requires teams of people with varying expertise. As a director, it gives me great pleasure to watch the departments across the museum come together and share ideas to create a dynamic and educational experience for our visitors. Matthew McLendon, Associate Curator of Modern and Contemporary Art, is to be commended for assembling these works for what is a new kind of exhibition for the museum that encourages new audiences to feel welcome and to see themselves reflected in the galleries.

**T. Marshall Rousseau**
Interim Director, The John and Mable Ringling Museum of Art

**GAJIN FUJITA**
*Chinita*, 2005, detail

# ACKNOWLEDGMENTS

The idea for this exhibition began germinating in my mind after viewing Mickalene Thomas's work at Art Basel Miami in 2007. I received early and enthusiastic encouragement from Jacqueline Bradley, who offered many important insights. I am most thankful to Jacqui and her husband, Clarence Otis, Jr., for sharing important works from their collection.

This exhibition and book would not have been possible without the enthusiastic support of the artists and the galleries that represent them. I am, of course, indebted to the artists, each of whom has been so generous in sharing their work and their thoughts in conversation. I am also deeply grateful to: Elizabeth East and LA Louver; Stephanie Smith and Kirsten Springer at Lehmann Maupin; Gail Host at Mickalene Thomas's studio; Claire Oliver and the Claire Oliver Gallery; Alberto Magnan, Dara Metz, and Lisa Friedman of Magnan Metz Gallery; Annie Galwak of G Fine Art; Brian Holcombe at Saltworks Gallery Atlanta; Elisabeth Sann at Jack Shainman Gallery; Kathryn Parker-Monteleone and the Rohna Hoffman Gallery; Krista Ware and Ray Hu of Kehinde Wiley's studio; Caren Golden of Caren Golden Fine Art, Janis Cecil at Marlborough, Lauren Rabb at The University of Arizona Museum of Art, and Dan Cameron at U.S. Biennial, Inc.

My colleagues at The John and Mable Ringling Museum of Art have offered support and encouragement at all stages of this project. Virginia Brilliant read early versions of the manuscript and, as always, offered invaluable insight and unerring critique. Françoise Hack, Ashley Burke, and Heidi Taylor in Registration assisted with the all-important practical logistics of the project without which nothing could be accomplished. Debbie Walk and Linda McKee also offered important editorial comments. Matthew Harmon, Aaron Board, and Donn Roll were instrumental in the success of the exhibition. Pam Fendt answered my many, many design questions and helped to make sure the resulting book is befitting of the works it contains. Dwight Currie offered encouragement and good humor, and enthusiastically collaborated on a hip-hop performance series in the Historic Asolo Theater to complement the exhibition. I would also like to thank T. Marshall Rousseau, Interim Director of The Ringling, and Sally McRorie, Dean of the College of Visual Arts, Theater and Dance at Florida State University, for providing me the opportunity to bring this work to the museum. The Board of Directors of the Museum, in particular Ina Schnell, has been most supportive as well. My graduate students in the *Beyond Bling* seminar at FSU were also helpful in shaping my ideas for the project. I learned as much, if not more, from them as they did from me, I am sure.

I would like to thank the entire Scala team who made this book a reality. Jennifer Wright Norman, Stephanie Emerson, Miko McGinty, Rita Jules, Anjali Pala, Gerard Mullin, Tim Clarke, Claudia Varosio, and Oliver Craske are all talented, consummate professionals who made me feel empowered and enabled at every step of the process. The incredibly short timeline we faced for this project seemed effortless in their capable hands. I have been very lucky to work with them.

I am most thankful to E. Luanne McKinnon and Eik Kahng—brilliant women, scholars, and curators whom I am lucky to call both mentors and friends. Each provides me unstinting encouragement, insight, and direction in all aspects of my work. Finally, I am eternally grateful to my family who support me unconditionally in every way.

**Matthew McLendon**
Associate Curator, Modern and Contemporary Art
The John and Mable Ringling Museum of Art

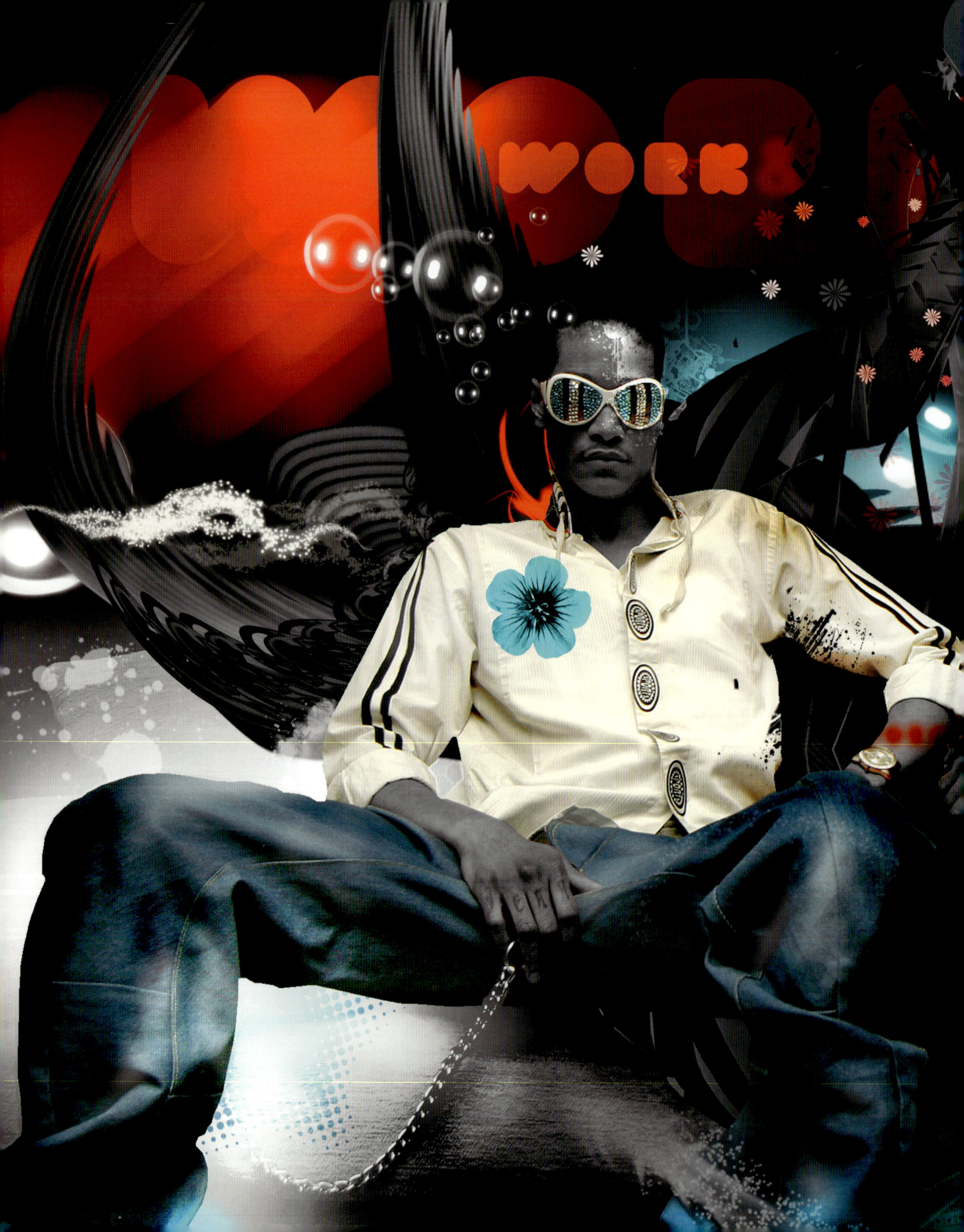
WORK

# COME AS YOU ARE

## Matthew McLendon

In his first-person account of the history of hip-hop, *Hip-Hop America*, the journalist and author Nelson George recounts a long Labor Day weekend on East Hampton in 1995 where he was surprised to see a performance by Run-D.M.C. He observes that the, "99.9 percent white audience knows the words to every song," and that, "the suburban crowd drinks, laughs, and tongue kisses with their heads pressed against booming speakers. It may not be what many folks want hip-hop to mean, but it is a true aspect of what hip-hop has become."[1] George's memory of that Labor Day succinctly demonstrates the pervasiveness of what has become one of the dominant cultural forces the world over. The present ubiquity of hip-hop, however, would have seemed an impossible fantasy for many of its proponents in the early years of the 1970s. That would all change, though, with a recording session in suburban New Jersey.

In October 2009, media outlets around the world marked the thirtieth anniversary of the release of the rap single largely credited with spreading rap, and the wider hip-hop culture of which it is a part, across America and, eventually, the world. Though not the first single to feature rap, the Sugarhill Gang's *Rapper's Delight* was the first to make the leap from the neighborhood to the nation. Its place on U.S. Pop and R&B charts (#36 and #4, respectively) demonstrated that rapping (MCing) could be packaged in the studio and successfully marketed to an audience outside New York's South Bronx, a concept largely derided before this by the earliest hip-hop artists. Now, as then, the disparity between what is packaged, commodified, and marketed to a "mainstream" audience and the far wider range of expressions that never make it out of the neighborhood, much less make it big, can be significant. Questions of the "authenticity" of mainstream hip-hop are still being debated. The Sugarhill Gang's story—three unknown rappers who had never been on stage, never performed live, and as the hip-hop journalist and historian Jeff Chang has observed, "wrote with the ears of fans and the enthusiasm of dilettantes"—is a telling preface to one that will recur throughout hip-hop's

**VINCE FRASER**
*Work & Play*, 2009, detail

history.[2] Yet, from their success, hip-hop has progressively become a dominant force not only within the practice of music and dance, but through the entirety of popular culture. Used to sell everything from the affordable Kia Soul via rapping hamsters outfitted in hoodies, bling, and the retro cool boombox, to premium liquors associated with the high-end luxury of the hip-hop lifestyle (Sean "Diddy" Combs and Cîroc Ultra Premium Vodka), hip-hop has proven itself an enduring and profitable brand as accepted in the living rooms of the manicured suburbs as it is on the streets of urban centers.

Although an established component of pop culture today, hip-hop emerged in the 1970s from a vortex of economic, social, and political turmoil largely situated in the Bronx borough of New York.[3] As an expressive outlet and money-maker for the disenfranchised youth in a crumbling inner city, hip-hop quickly became a way of life incorporating its own linguistic and visual signifiers. Early on, four main components of hip-hop expression came together in symbiosis. MCing (rapping), Djing (spinning), B-boying (break dancing), and graffiti were the potent ingredients that would combine in various ratios to form a hip-hop happening.

Through graffiti, hip-hop has always had a strong visual component. As a transgressive act of social defiance, graffiti was the perfect visual complement to the verbal critiques of hip-hop's MCs. Graffiti's aesthetic of trope—building one's style on existing examples of calligraphic design, but then modifying and personalizing the appropriation— paralleled the sampling of fragments of music woven by the DJs into complex aural webs upon which the MCs layered their words. Graffiti's *Rapper's Delight* moment came in 1983 with the release of Tony Silver's and Henry Chalfant's documentary *Style Wars*. While the film included sequences of rapping and break dancing, the emphasis was clearly on graf and featured some of the most important innovators in the field such as Futura, Iz the Wiz, and Zephyr. With the subsequent publication of the books *Subway Art* (Martha Cooper and Henry Chalfant, 1984), and the follow-up *Spray Can Art* (Henry Chalfant and James Prigoff, 1987), graffiti gained nation-wide attention as did the very heated debate between Mayor Ed Koch, who viewed the graffiti covered New York subway cars as casualties of vandalism, and the graf artists and their supporters, who viewed them as the ultimate expression of urban art.

Graffiti had already been translated on a limited scale into the gallery through the works of a few pioneering artists, including the artists' collective Collaborative Projects (Colab). In 1980 Colab turned a disused massage parlor in Times Square into *The Times Square Show*, a massive exhibition with works by Jean-Michel Basquiat, Keith Haring, and Kenny Scharf among others. The exhibition opened the way for each of these artists, in their own time, to take a street aesthetic into the galleries. It is unsurprising, then, that thirty plus years on, hip-hop has come to be a significant voice within contemporary visual art.

By the early 2000s, a number of high profile exhibitions exploring hip-hop's influence on art were being mounted. The Brooklyn Museum's multi-media exhibition *Hip-Hop Nation: Roots, Rhyme, and Rage* in 2000 took a somewhat anthropological approach, studying the rise of hip-hop from the early 1970s through to the "golden age" of hip-hop in the 1990s. Featuring fashions worn by some of the genre's biggest names, as well as handwritten lyrics, industry magazines, and a limited range of art associated with hip-hop, the exhibition was largely criticized for being too tame. Roberta Smith lamented in *The New York Times* that, "this show feels like a cross between a mall and a mausoleum; it simultaneously panders to its audience and isolates its subject from both its own vitality and its broader cultural context."[4] The intention of the curator, the journalist Kevin Powell, of "recognizing that this art form, which has grown from an attitude to a culture, is now the chief way young people communicate all over the globe," was laudable.[5] Yet in the eyes of many critics, the Brooklyn Museum's attempt to "legitimize" hip-hop as a significant cultural phenomenon by embracing it within the walls of the museum, fell prey to the danger of trying to translate the movement's raw, live energy through the display of memorabilia—itself the empty shell of a past moment.

But other exhibitions focusing on the visual and performing artists influenced by hip-hop would quickly follow. *One Planet Under a Groove: Hip-Hop and Contemporary Art*, the 2001 exhibition at The Bronx Museum of the Arts, explicitly considered hip-hop's influence on contemporary art. The exhibition's curators, Lydia Yee and Franklin Sirmans, took a broad view of art produced between 1980 and the new millennium in order to "explore a wide range of issues, including style and identity, social and political concerns, aesthetics, black vernacular culture, and historical precedents and future directions as well as inherent contradictions, which are all a part of the fabric of hip-hop culture."[6] By 2000 it was clear that the historiography of hip-hop needed serious consideration, and Yee's and Sirman's exhibition, which contained work by thirty artists hailing not only from New York but also California, Texas, Europe, and Japan, made a powerful statement about the movement's role in the creative lives of the artists, many of whom had never known a world without hip-hop. *One Planet Under a Groove* was quite prescient in its bold linking of a mass-appeal movement and art produced for the gallery or museum context. *The New York Times*' Roberta Smith was far more generous in her appraisal of this hip-hop exhibition noting that, "with minimal resources, and maximum diversity, [the exhibition] has roughed out much of the scope of its subject."[7]

While not explicitly exploring hip-hop's relationship to contemporary art, Thelma Golden's 2001 exhibition *Freestyle* at The Studio Museum in Harlem included work by twenty-eight African American artists, many of whom were in their thirties and, thus, firmly a part of what might be called the "hip-hop generation." Yet, Golden herself vehemently denied this characterization. Talking with *The Village Voice*'s Greg Tate the afternoon of the opening of the exhibition she asserted, "the one thing I was adamant about was not creating a hip-hop show. Because I am the holdout that believes there is no hip-hop corollary in visual art... One thing I thought was, what happens in a moment when popular culture is so present—and within popular culture hip-hop is ever present—when you do a show of emerging African American artists? I'm waiting to see the tag lines and headlines because I guarantee one of them is going to say, 'Hip-hop Generation.'"[8] But Tate states that, "The mark of hip-hop is everywhere in *Freestyle*—formally, semiotically, referentially, from the name on."[9] This disparity of opinions between intention and reception illustrates an important point. As late as 2001, hip-hop's embrace by the keepers of one aspect of cultural validation—the notion of "high art" as enshrined and enabled by the museum—was still, at best, tenuous. Though many had argued that by this point hip-hop had "sold out" and was a corporatized cipher of its initial self, its roots and continued existence as a mass movement of popular expression seemed to be present enough to keep it, at least in the eyes of one of the most prominent African-American curators working in the United States, at a distance from the aura of vanguardism the exhibition sought to establish. Unlike the art in *One Planet Under a Groove*, which was proffered as existing within a larger hip-hop paradigm, *Freestyle* sought to disengage the displayed work from the most overwhelming cultural *zeitgeist* for most, if not all, of its artists. A one-to-one corollary between hip-hop and art is certainly facile, yet, as Derek Conrad Murray assessed, "there is a corollary between hip-hop's worldview and the worldview of the artists."[10]

Almost a decade has passed since these first important exhibitions explored the genealogies and influences of hip-hop both on mass culture and the vanguard of art, and hip-hop has continued as a potent and pervasive multi-billion dollar industry. While the exhibition that accompanies this book is in no way meant as a comprehensive panorama of hip-hop's influence in art in all realms, it is intended as an entrée into work being produced now, by a group of artists as diverse as hip-hop itself—a snapshot of a moment in time. East Coast and West Coast are represented. African American, Latino/a-American, Japanese American, and European voices make up the chorus; two of the artists are openly gay; and four of the ten are women. These individuals are presented not simply as "hip-hop artists," but rather as a cross-section of artists working at the vanguard of contemporary practice who are actively influenced by and contributing to the evolution of our notions of hip-hop and street culture expressions. This art is now—nothing more, nothing less.

---

The work of Michael Anderson, like hip-hop, comes from the street. Anderson constructs large-scale works collaged entirely from street posters he has collected the world over. The tension created in the highly patterned backgrounds (as in *Israeli Hip Hop* for example), often resembles the near Abstract-Expressionist experience of the graffiti-covered walls from which the posters came. The density of the images, the visual cacophony of layer upon layer of image and meaning mimics the visual overload of the city street. Anderson's collages are the equivalent of the hip-hop DJ who makes a reputation by pulling together as disparate samples as possible into a cohesive aural experience. Speaking of collage in terms of "collecting," Michael Anderson's work is filled with simultaneous juxtapositions of global pop culture.

**MICHAEL ANDERSON**
*Tropical Fantasy*, 2010
Street poster collage
44 x 57 inches
Image courtesy of Claire Oliver | New York

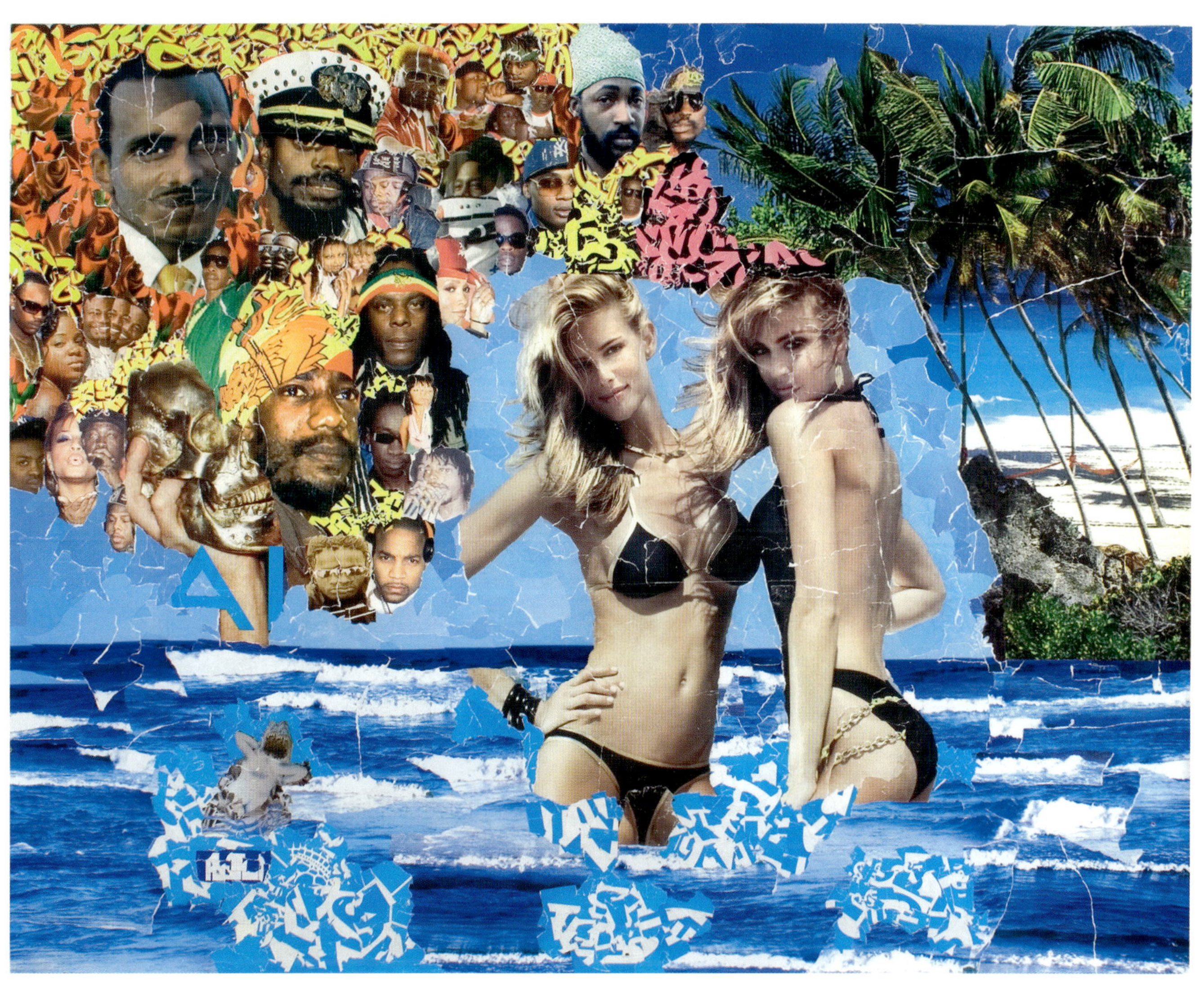

**MICHAEL ANDERSON**
*Israeli Hip Hop*, 2004
Street poster collage
20½ x 15¾ inches
Image courtesy of Claire Oliver | New York

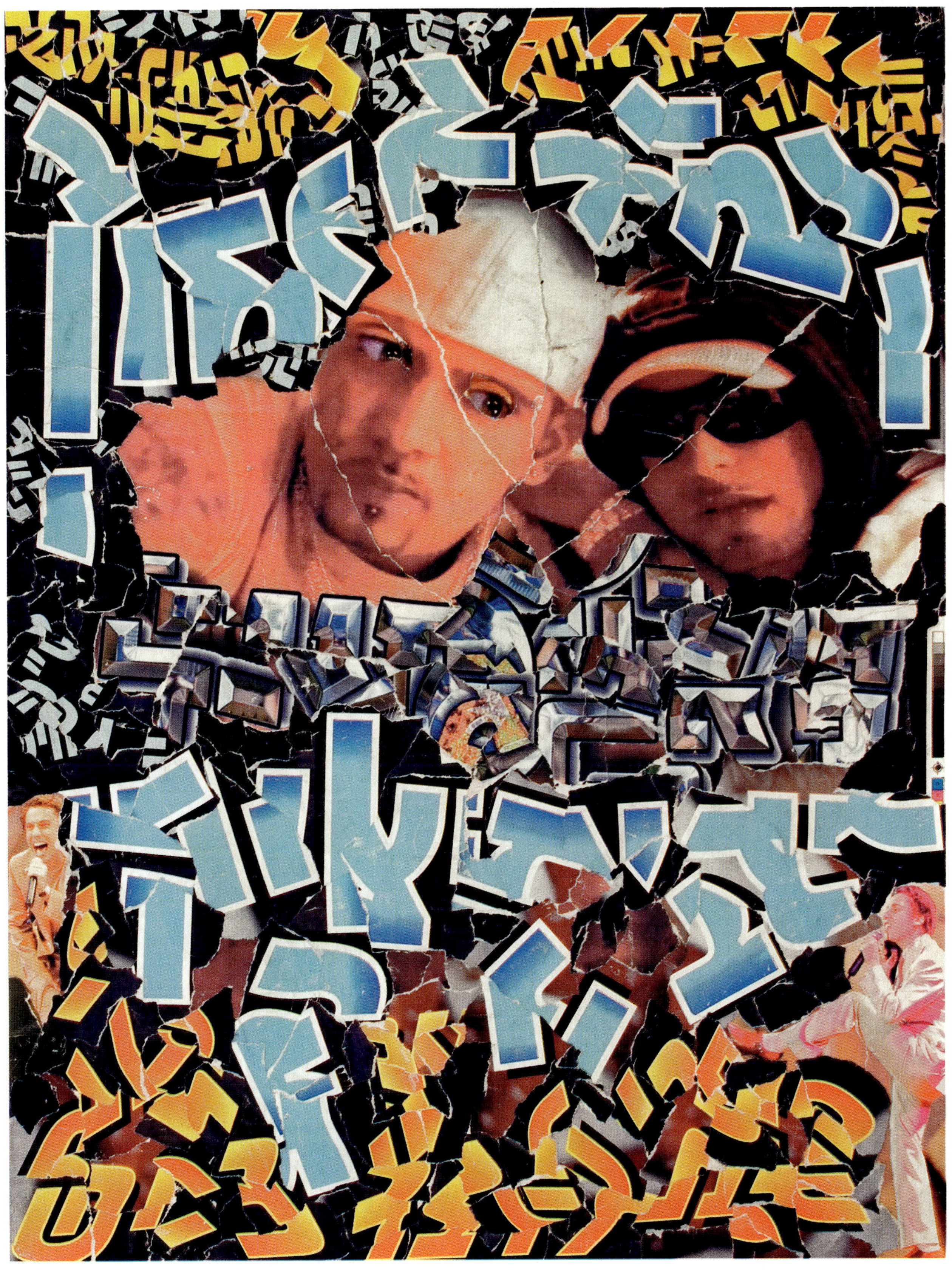

**MICHAEL ANDERSON**
*The Five Deadly Venoms*, 2005
Street poster collage
96 x 96 inches
Image courtesy of Claire Oliver | New York

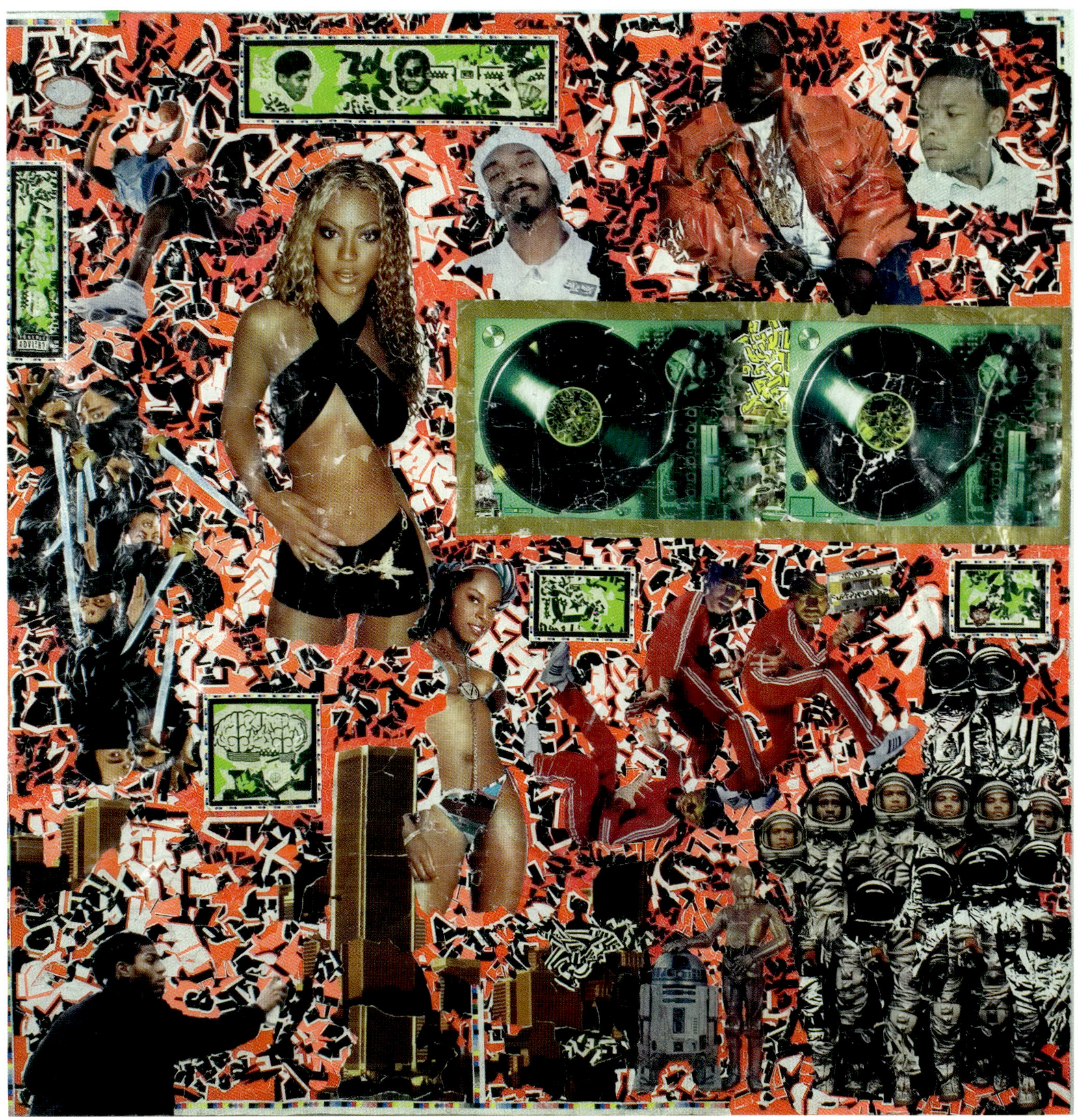

**MICHAEL ANDERSON**
*Black Music vs. Helvetica*, 2009
Street poster collage
Polyptych of 4 panels
120 x 144 inches
Image courtesy of Claire Oliver | New York
(detail following pages)

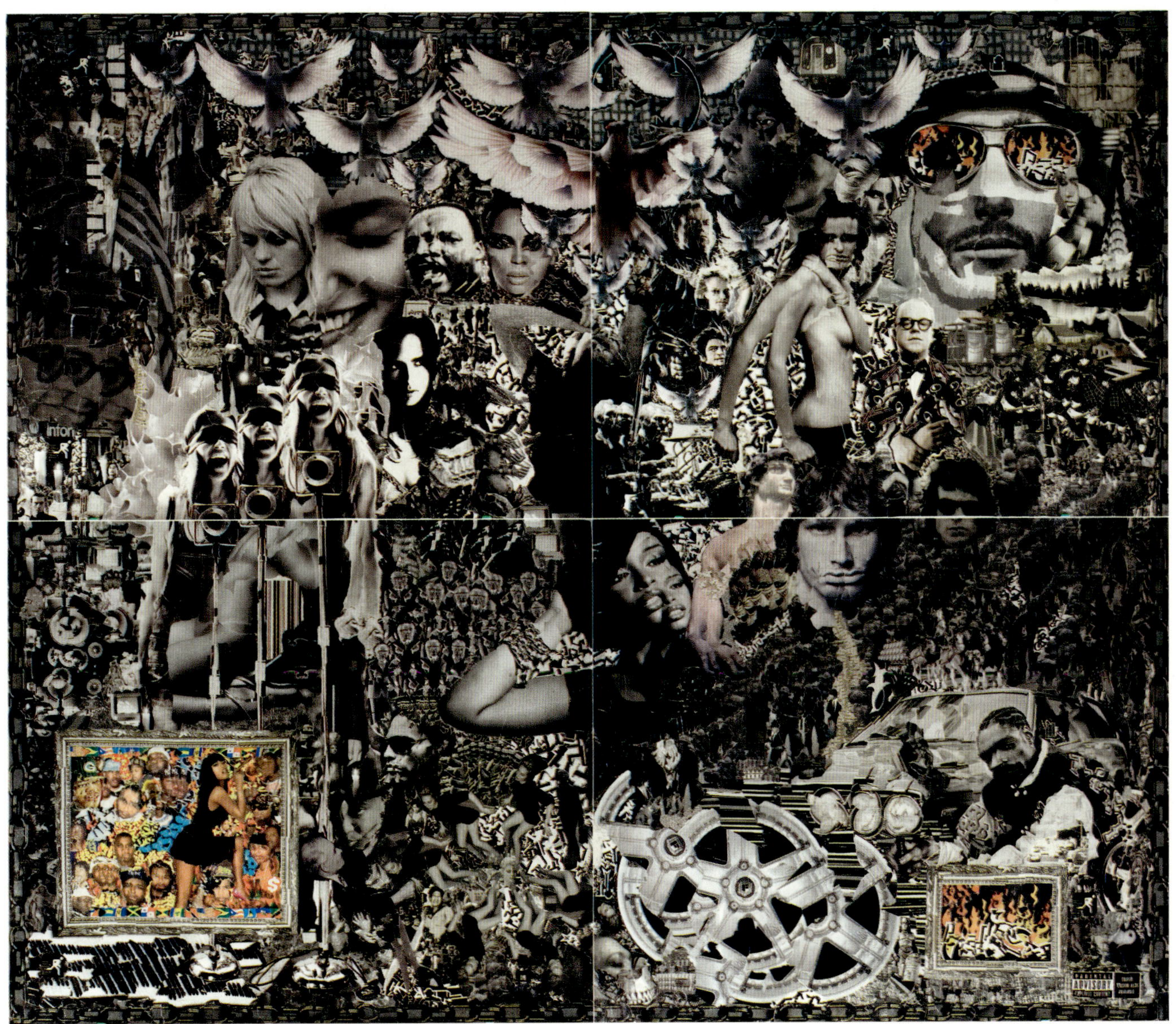

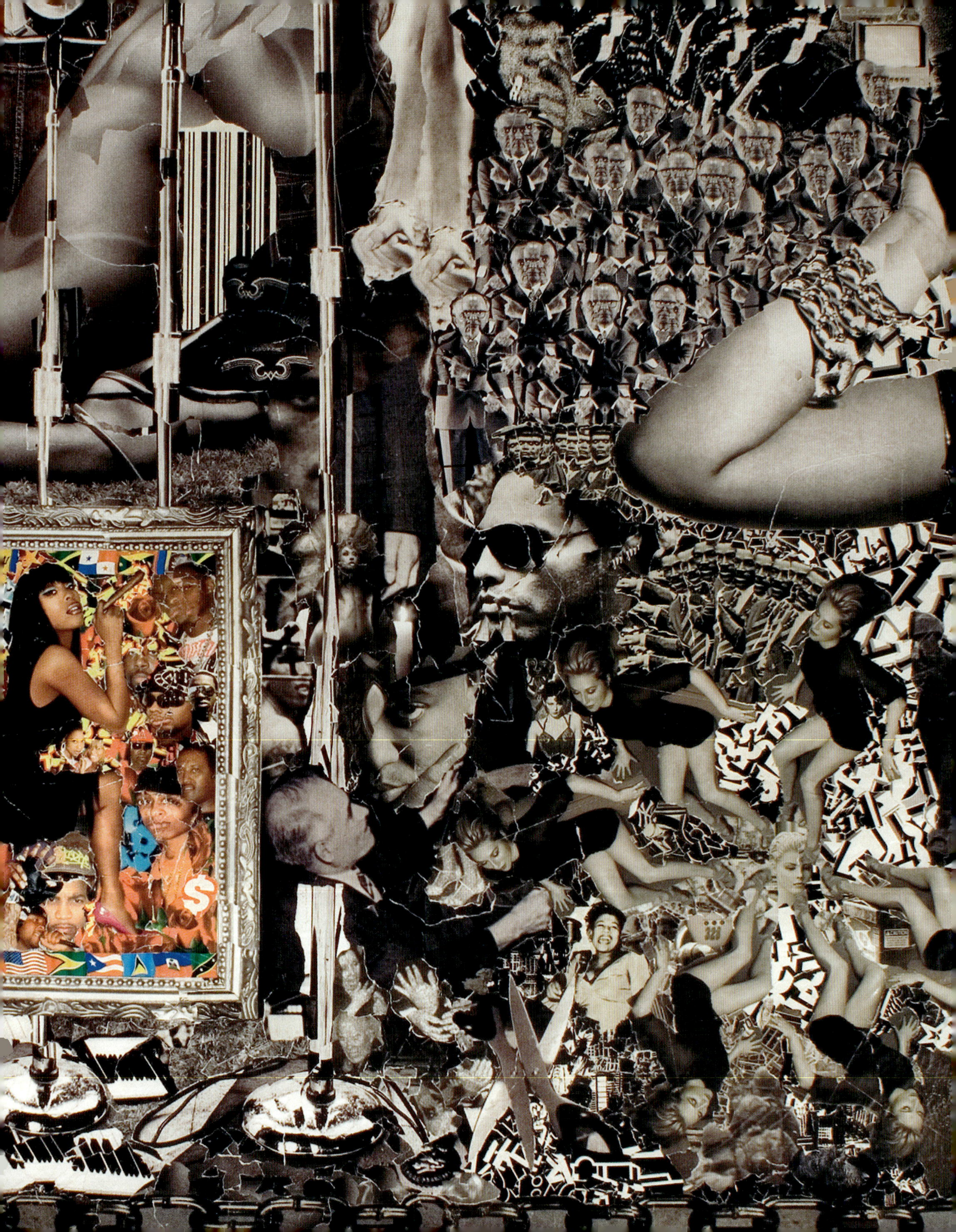

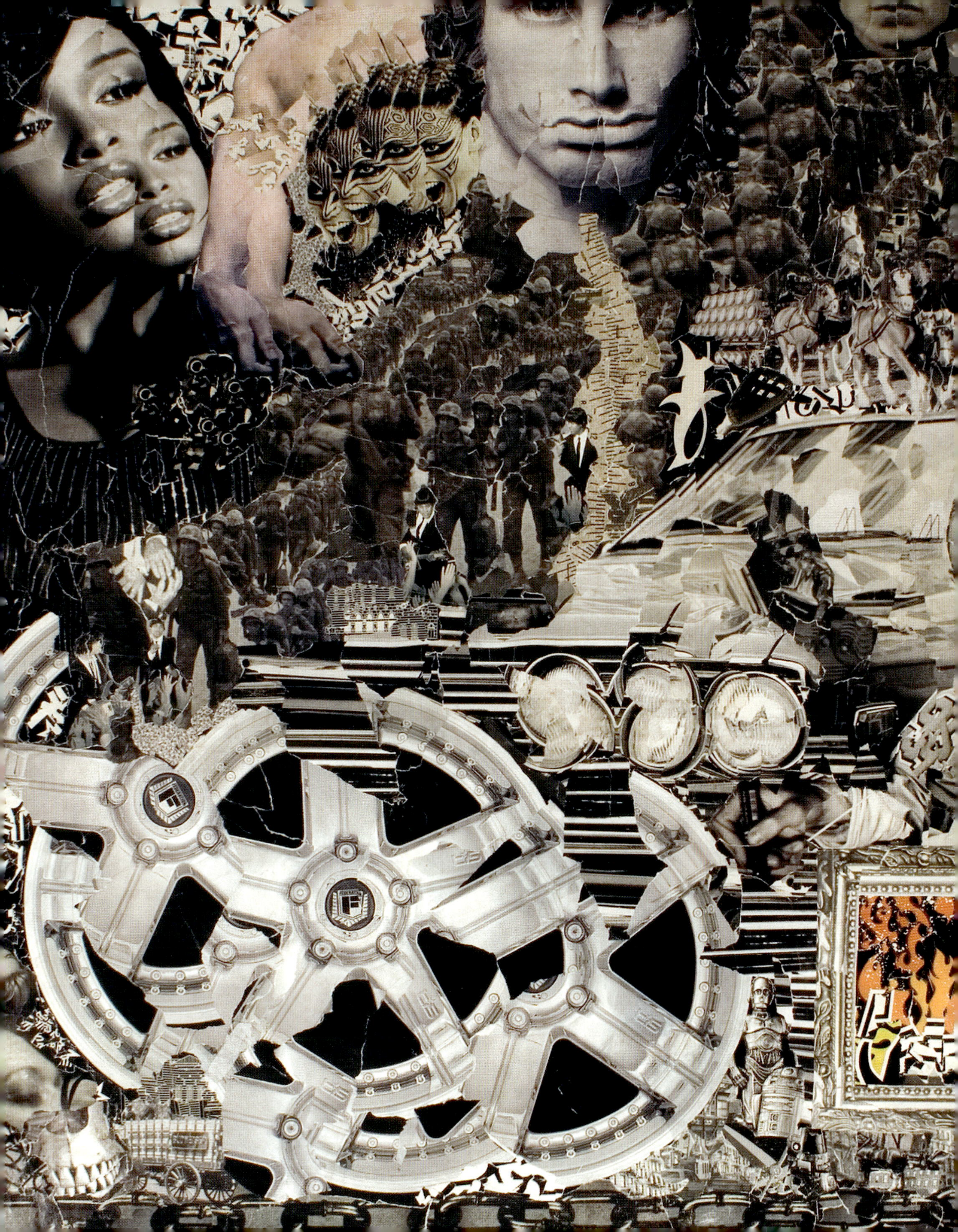

No work better illustrates this than *The Five Deadly Venoms*, 2005, in which hip-hop celebrity Snoop Dogg, the DJs' turntables, the hip-hop video girls, the tracksuits, the bling are placed alongside *Star Wars* characters R2D2 and C-3PO. The juxtaposition clearly suggests that these two aspects of popular culture—one which might be stereotyped as African American and one which may be read as white and even suburban—are part of a larger indivisible expression of global culture that "samples" from all expressions. Anderson's collage mosaics frequently juxtapose Caucasian and African American celebrities such as in the monumental *Black Music vs. Helvetica*, 2009, in which Jim Morrison and Philip Seymour Hoffman come together with Dr. Martin Luther King, Jr., and Snoop Dogg all under the spreading wings of the dove of peace. Referring to the complexity of such an image, Anderson suggests he is constructing, "non-linear narratives . . . that can follow a number of story lines in any given collage," and links this with changing television channels and surfing the World Wide Web.[11] That these collages are created from street posters—that is, advertisements—must also be taken into account. By using the most visible tool of consumption as source material, Anderson's collages repurpose the quotidian visual landscape of material desire, thereby forcing, through recontextualization a new appraisal of mass-market imagery.

At times, as in *Tropical Fantasy* and *The Five Deadly Venoms*, desire continues to be a strong, overt component. The men of *Tropical Fantasy* desire the women who appear as if a mirage of sexual fantasy or a Venus rising from the sea. Anderson resists, however, any reading that this depiction negatively objectifies the woman. Alternately, he suggests that these are, "the rich beautiful women who go to the islands to find a quick fun lover and then leave," and thus places the power of the narrative in the women.[12] In *Black Music vs. Helvetica*, desire recedes but is still present in the pop of color in the lower left corner as well as in references to material culture, the *David*, the tire rims, and the car. His *Israeli Hip Hop*, 2004, is not about the desire of a woman or the desire of the material, but rather the desire of these young hip-hop artists to affect the style of their American forebears, thus legitimizing their claim to the hip-hop experience.

While Michael Anderson takes his material directly from the street, the work of Los Angeles–based artist Gajin Fujita combines the graffiti practice he experienced as a youth growing up in the East Los Angeles neighborhood of Boyle Heights along with traditional *ukiyo-e* imagery associated with his Japanese heritage. Graffiti has been a strong force within contemporary art since the 1970s when it started to be recognized as a fully realized aesthetic statement, not wanton vandalism. As it has matured in the collective consciousness of the art world, the aesthetics of graffiti have constantly been referenced, re-worked, and manipulated in any number of ways. As a member of the graffiti crews KGB (Kids Gone Bad) and then KIIS (Kill To Succeed) in his teen years, Fujita was immersed in the mostly friendly rivalry between crews that constantly looked to one-up the other through ever more elaborate designs and typographic innovations.

For large works such as *The Saints*, 2008, Fujita invites friends from his days as a graffiti artist to tag the panels of the work using them as "studio assistants."[13] The panels, variously covered in gold, silver, or platinum leaf replicating the surfaces of the traditional subway car "canvases" for graffiti, simultaneously operate as defaced objects of luxury as well as the support for the dynamic, highly rendered scenes of Fujita's creation. Referencing the professional football team that has become a rallying point for hope and aspiration in post-Katrina New Orleans, the central figure—a kabuki-inspired samurai adorned with the fleurs-de-lis and gold, purple, and green associated with the Crescent City—may be read as referring to the "team" of the graffiti crew as well as the vaunted position of the post-modern warrior status that professional athletes are afforded in a contemporary culture infused with the hip-hop love of logos (themselves a type of "tag"). The conspicuous signs of allegiances, often predicated on location or neighborhoods reinforced here by the area codes 213 and 504 for L.A. and New Orleans, respectively, draw the parallel between the history of the feudal Japanese warriors beholden to land-owning nobles and the fidelity to the crews, gangs and sports teams of the contemporary urban experience with its own politicized geographies.[14]

**GAJIN FUJITA**
*The Saints*, 2008
Gold leaf, acrylic, spray paint, and paint marker on wood panel
Six panels
72 x 108 inches overall
U.S. Biennial Inc/Prospect New Orleans, courtesy of LA Louver, Venice, CA

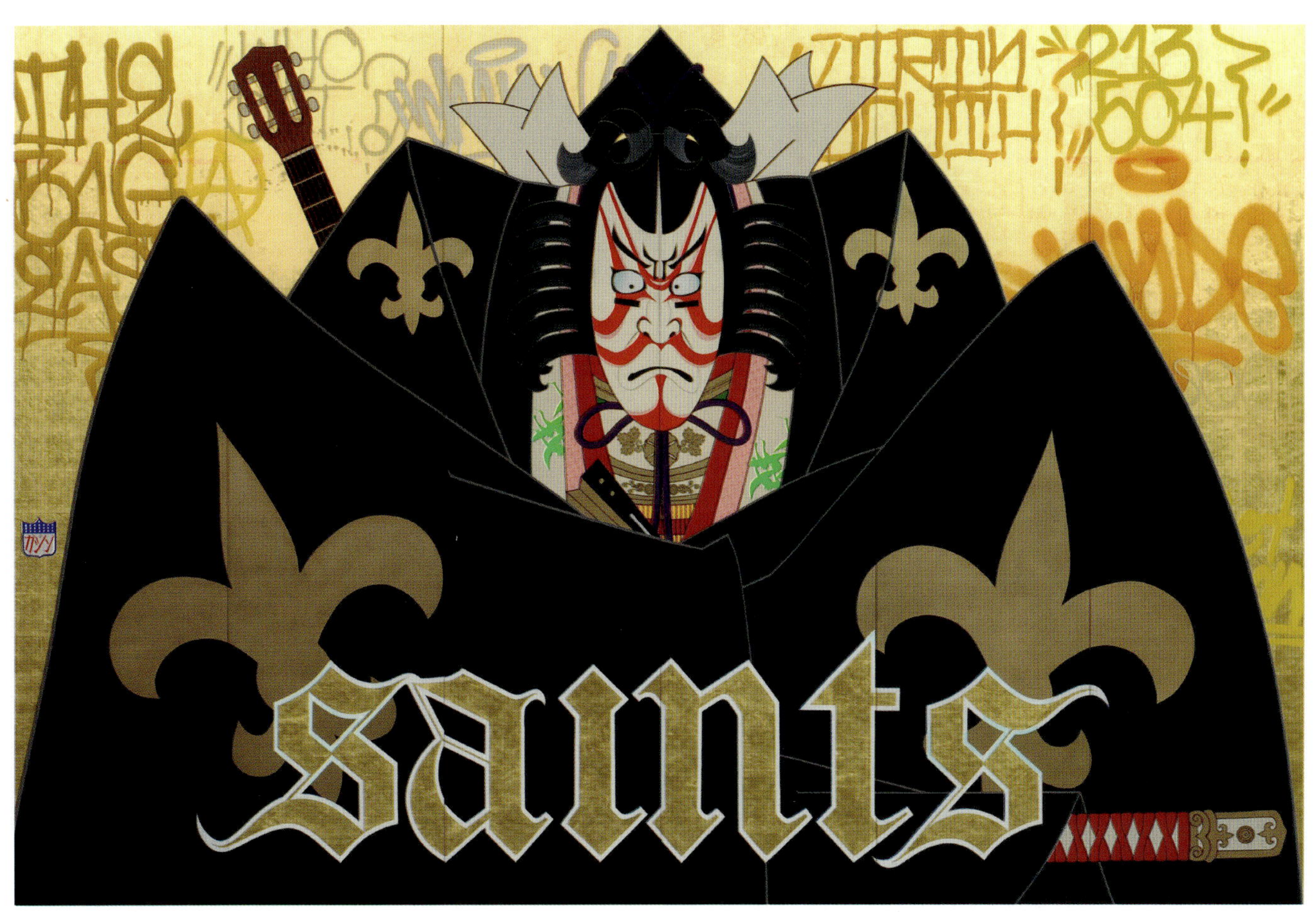
saints

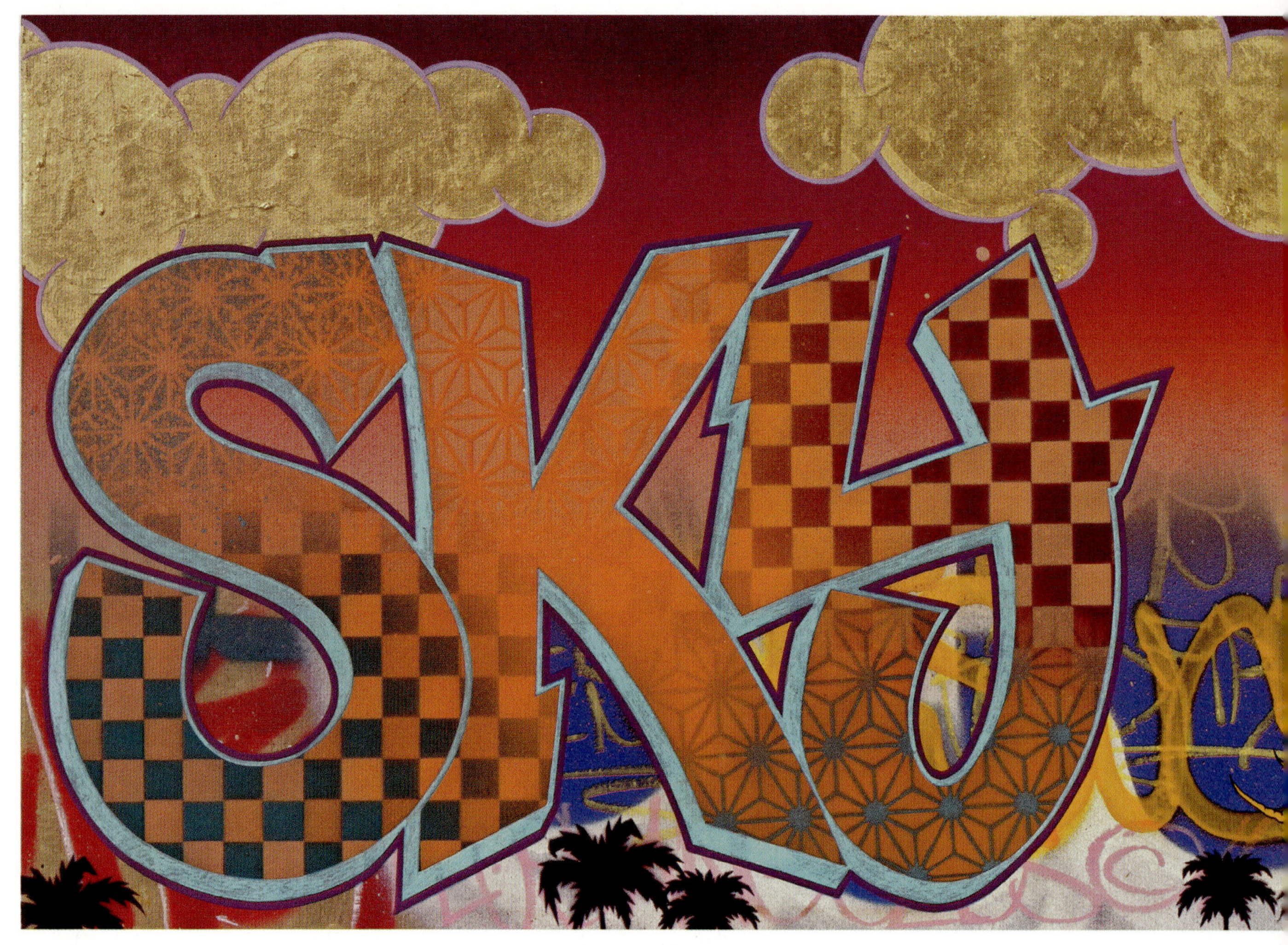


**GAJIN FUJITA**
*Sky High*, 2007
Gold leaf, acrylic, paint marker, spray paint, and Mean Streak on panel
16 x 48 inches
Courtesy of LA Louver, Venice, CA
(detail following pages)

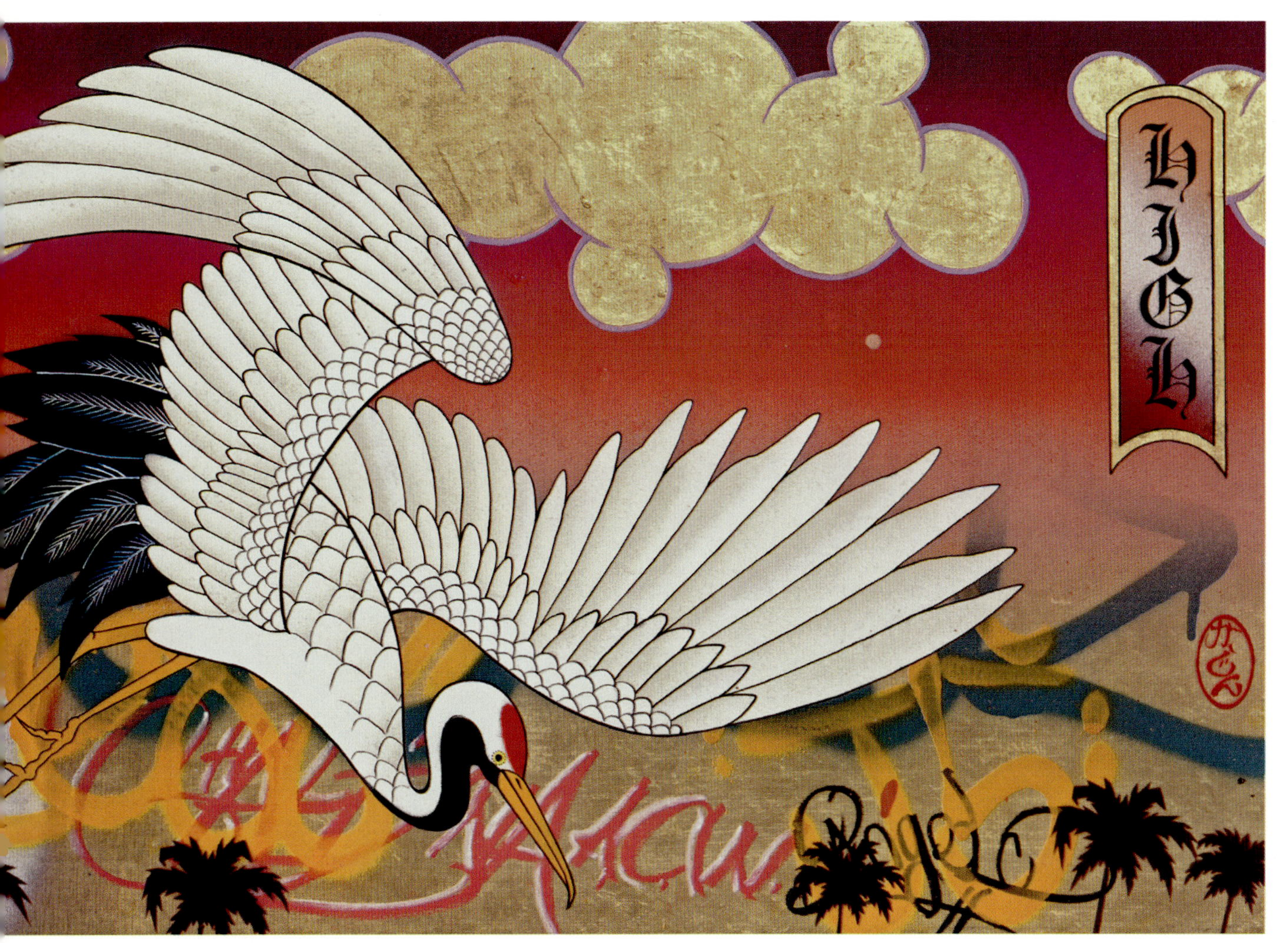
HIGH

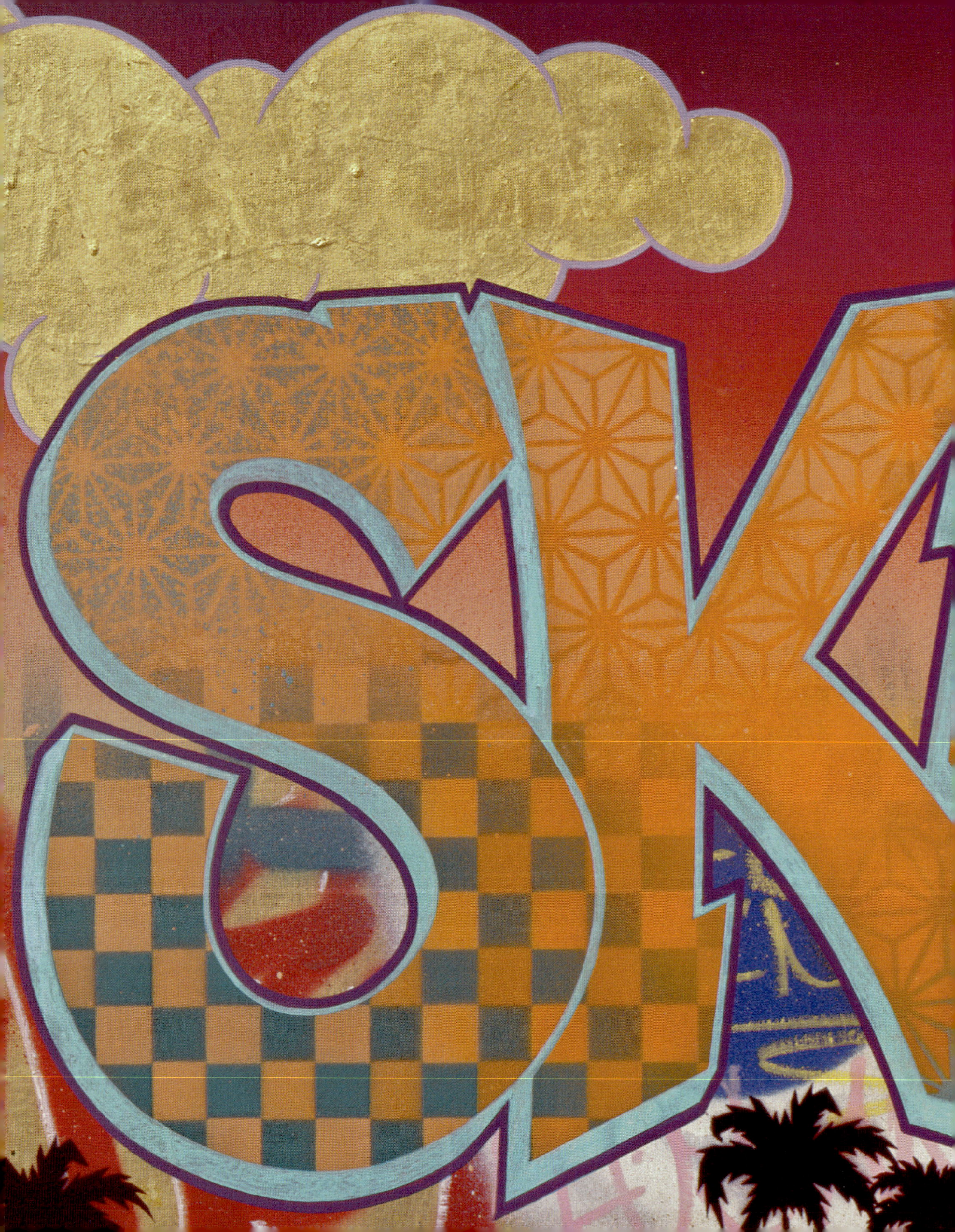

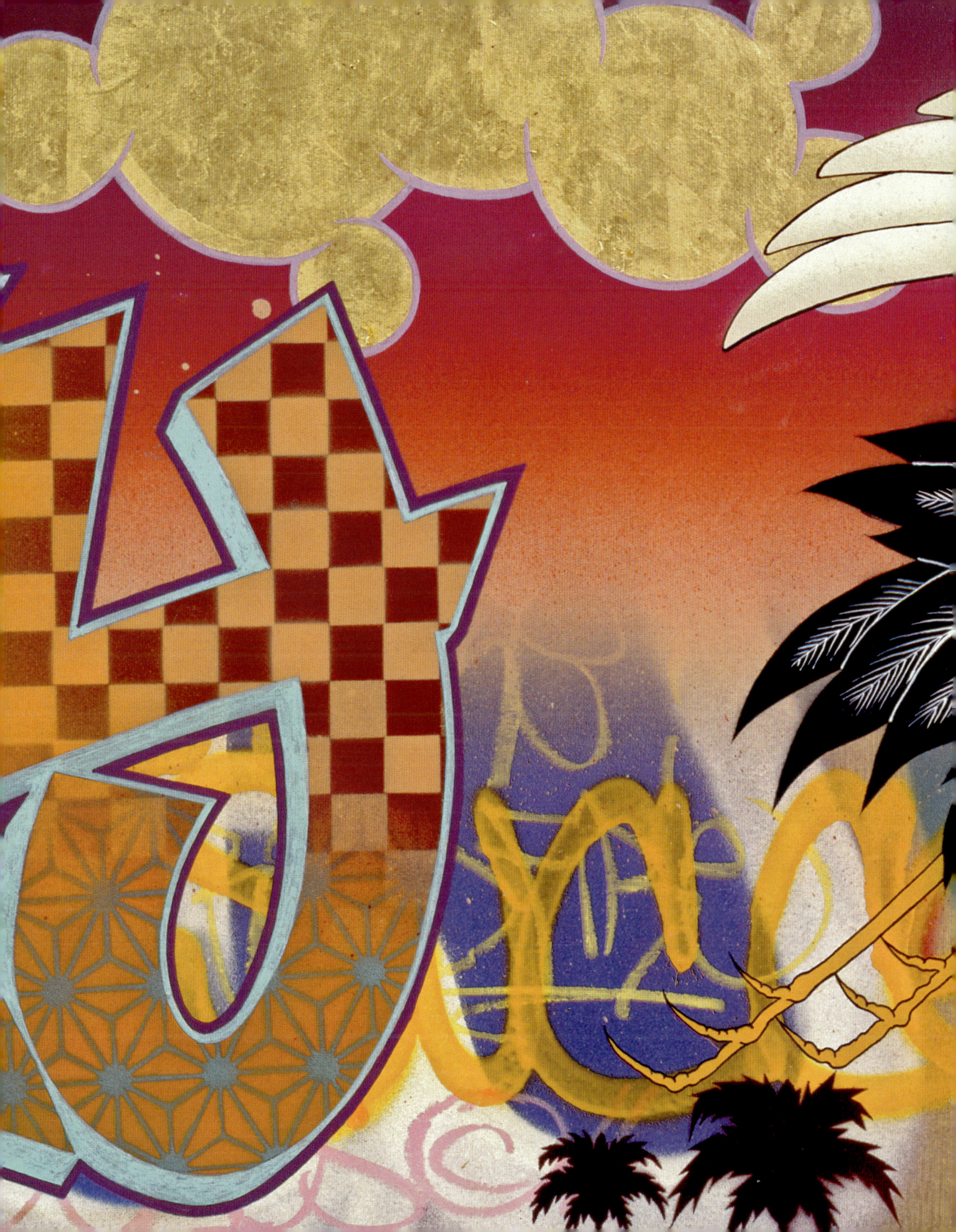

**GAJIN FUJITA**
*Chinita*, 2005
Platinum leaf, acrylic, spray paint, Mean Streak, and paint marker on wood panel
24 x 16 inches
Private collection, courtesy of LA Louver, Venice, CA

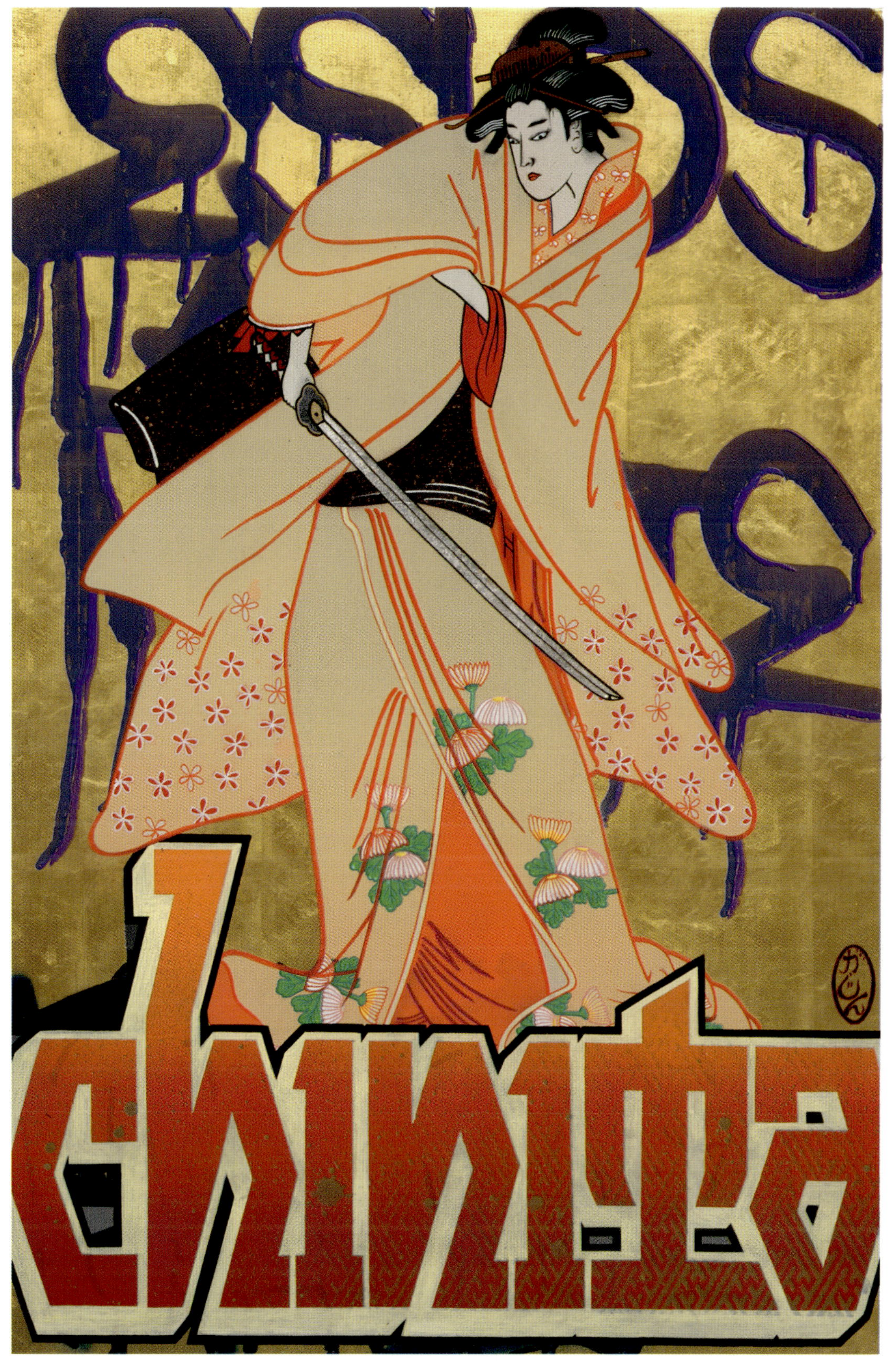

**iona rozeal brown**
*divine selektah . . . big up [after yoshitoshi's moon of the filial son]*, 2006
Acrylic and gold leaf on panel
61 x 49¾ inches
Museum Purchase with funds provided by Robert J. Greenberg; acc. No. 2006.005.001
Collection of the University of Arizona Museum of Art & Archive of Visual Arts

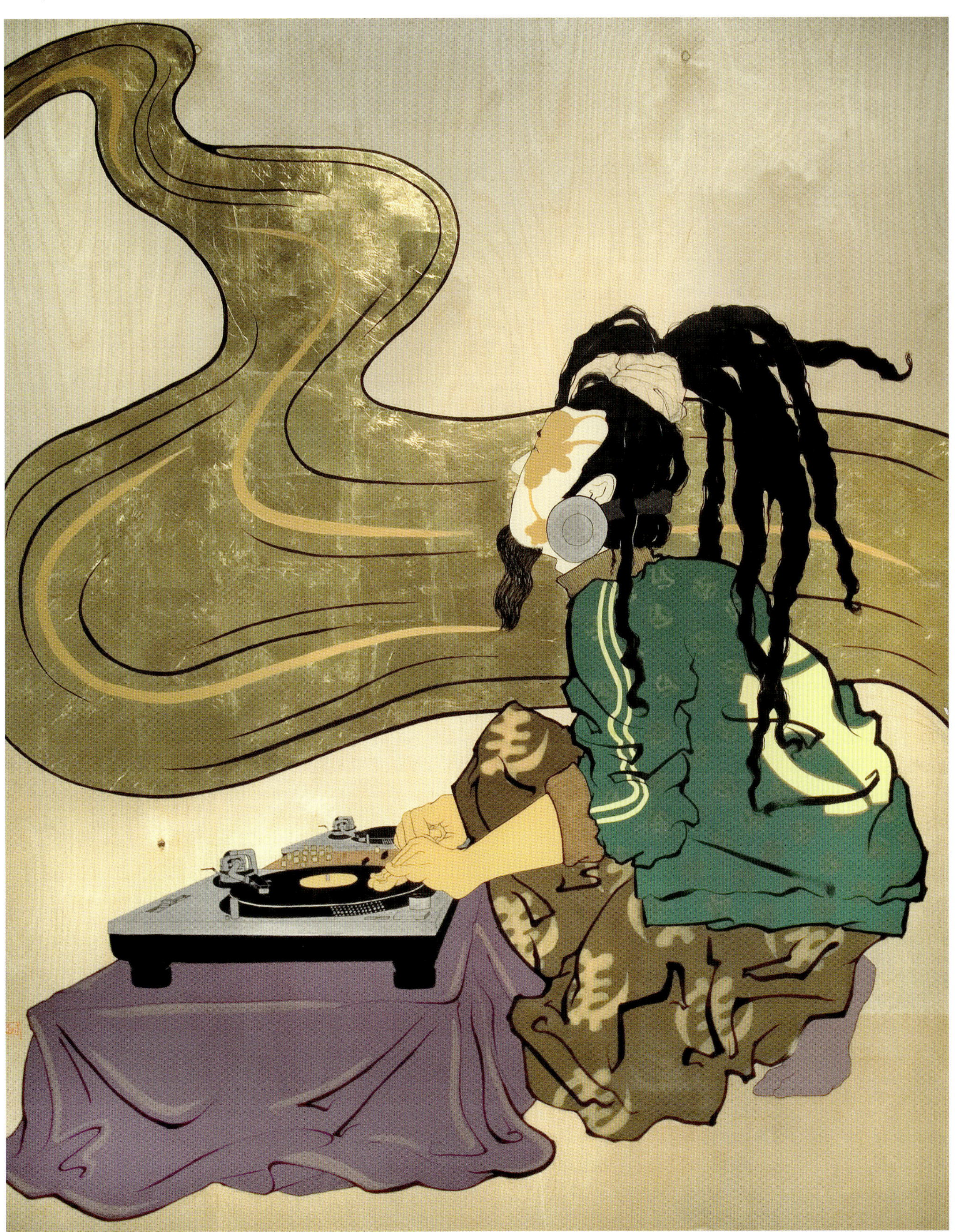

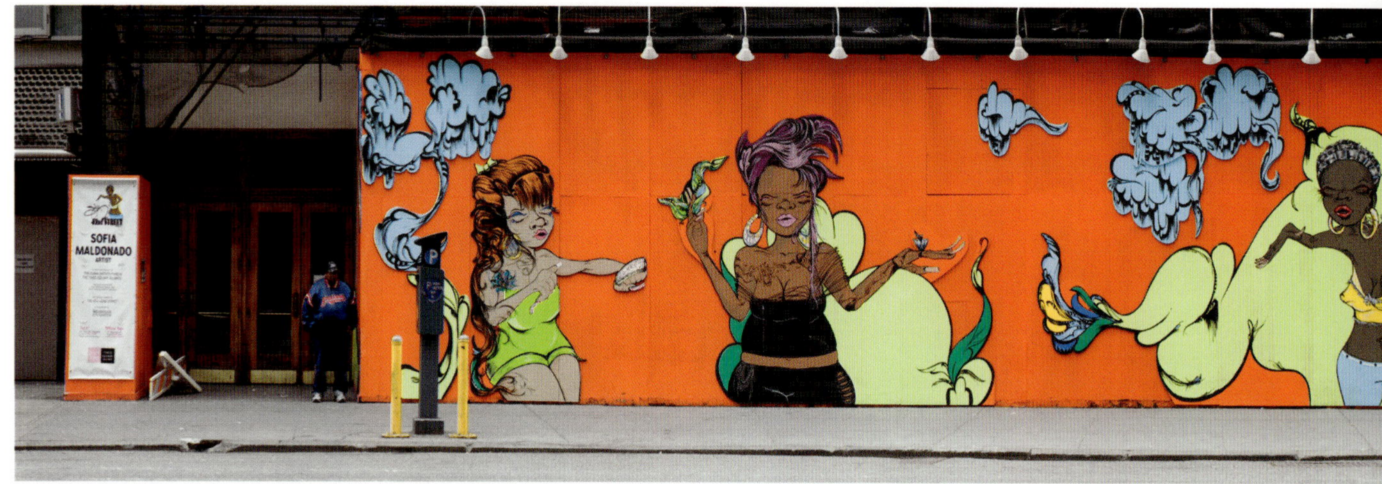


**SOFIA MALDONADO**
42nd Street mural
Courtesy of Magnan Metz Gallery, New York
(detail following pages)

In recent works, Fujita has also employed the sexually provocative imagery of the print genres *shunga* (spring pictures) and *bijin-ga* (pictures of beautiful women). As Elizabeth Dunbar has pointed out, "the women depicted [in these genres] were no mere prostitutes; rather, these courtesans and geishas were highly sophisticated companions."[15] In *Chinita*, 2005, Fujita may again be seen simultaneously sampling from a Japanese past and a contemporary culture with strong consonances with that past. This "beautiful woman" has a harder edge, literally, than her historic precedents as she brandishes the samurai sword and stands before the letters ESLOS leaving no doubt that she is East Side tough. The mix of historic and contemporary cultures is furthered by her emphatic identification as a *chinita*, urban Spanish parlance for an Asian woman or a woman with Asian and Latino heritage. Appearing on a panel of platinum leaf measuring just 24 x 16 inches, this *chinita* is offered up for private delectation, but asserts herself with the flourish of her sword from beneath her cherry-blossom pink robes.

Another artist looking to the parallels between Edo culture and the contemporary world of hip-hop is iona rozeal brown, who has based a number of works on the contemporary Japanese phenomenon of *ganguro*. In *ganguro* (literally "black face"), predominately young women sport deep brown tans accentuated with dark eyeliner and contrasting white lipstick in an attempt to mimic the dramatic styles of African American hip-hop divas. Initially angered by the superficial appropriation of aspects of black hip-hop culture by Japanese teenagers with no interest in its history or social ramifications, brown

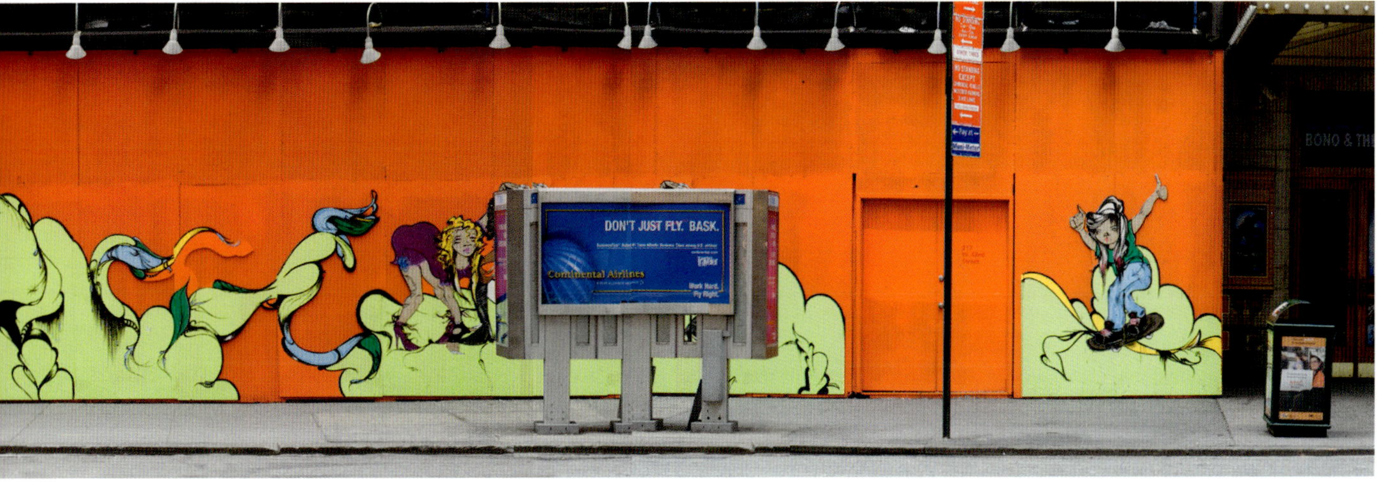


eventually came to see *ganguro* as an act of rebellion and identity construction by Japanese teenage girls chaffing at the social restrictions placed upon them by a traditional society.[16] In work like *divine selektah . . . big up [after yoshitoshi's moon of the filial son]*, 2006, brown conflates the influence of Tsukioka Yoshitoshi (1839–1892, a master of *ukiyo-e* prints), the contemporary Japanese appropriation of aspects of hip-hop signifiers, and her response as an African American woman living in the wider context of hip-hop culture in America. Within the wider picture, brown's interaction with *ganguro* demonstrates hip-hop's pervasiveness throughout the world. Further, while the adherents of *ganguro* may have little to no interest in the wider historical implications of "blackface," by appropriating signifiers of what the Japanese deem black hip-hop culture, the revolutionary and defiant aspects of hip-hop, arguably now historic in the American context, are recovered and translated to a new cultural paradigm.

The depiction of women in hip-hop culture is complicated at best. While there were relatively early examples of successful female hip-hop artists like the duo Salt N' Peppa or Queen Latifah, who has been successful in crossing over into television, film, and modeling, the criticism of the objectification and sexualization of women has remained a constant leitmotif within, and more often outside of, hip-hop culture. Michael Anderson, Gajin Fujita, and iona rozeal brown have each approached this to varying degrees. With her recent mural commission by the Times Square Alliance for 42nd Street in Times Square, Sofia Maldonado found herself squarely within this ongoing debate.

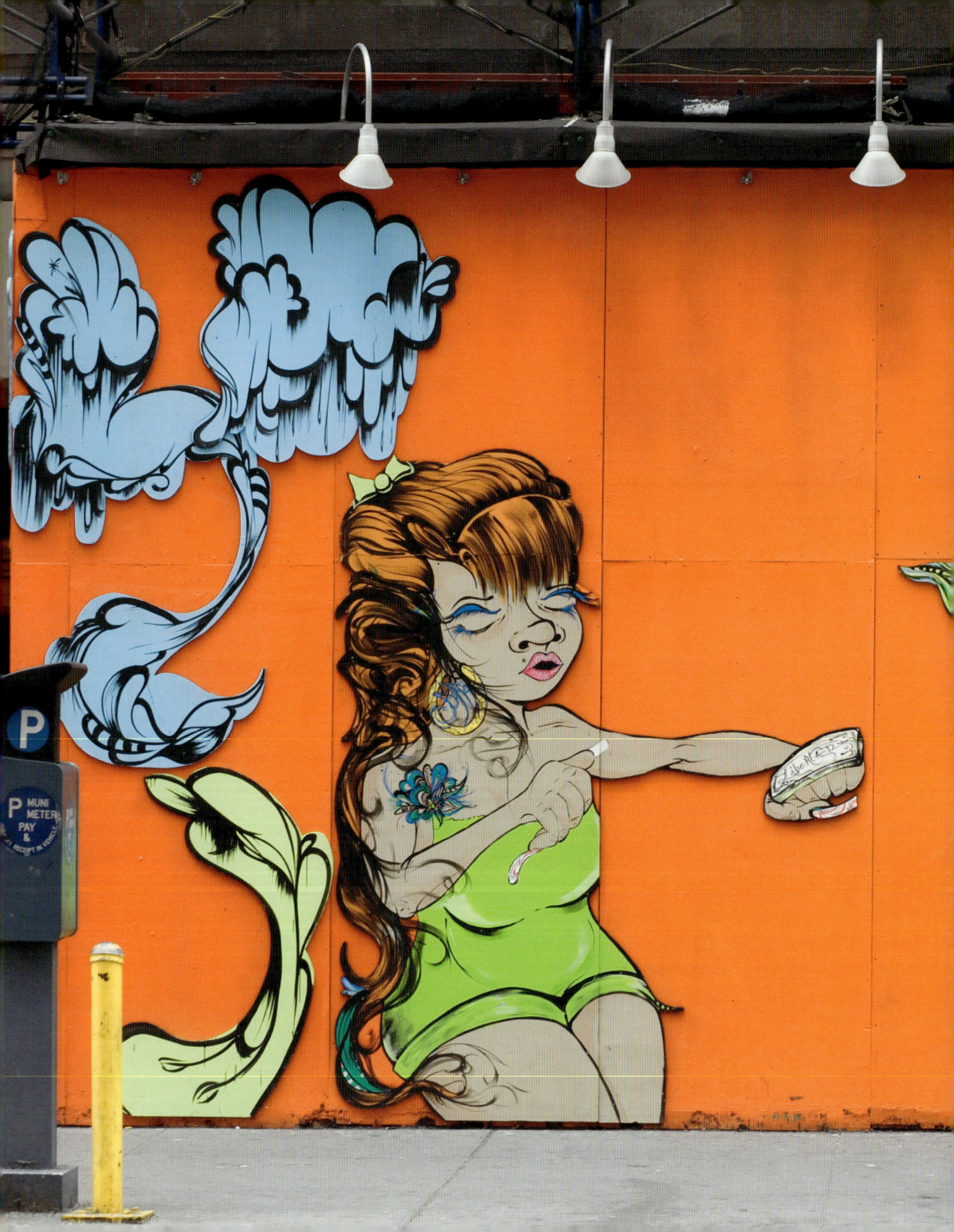
P
P MUNI METER
PAY
&

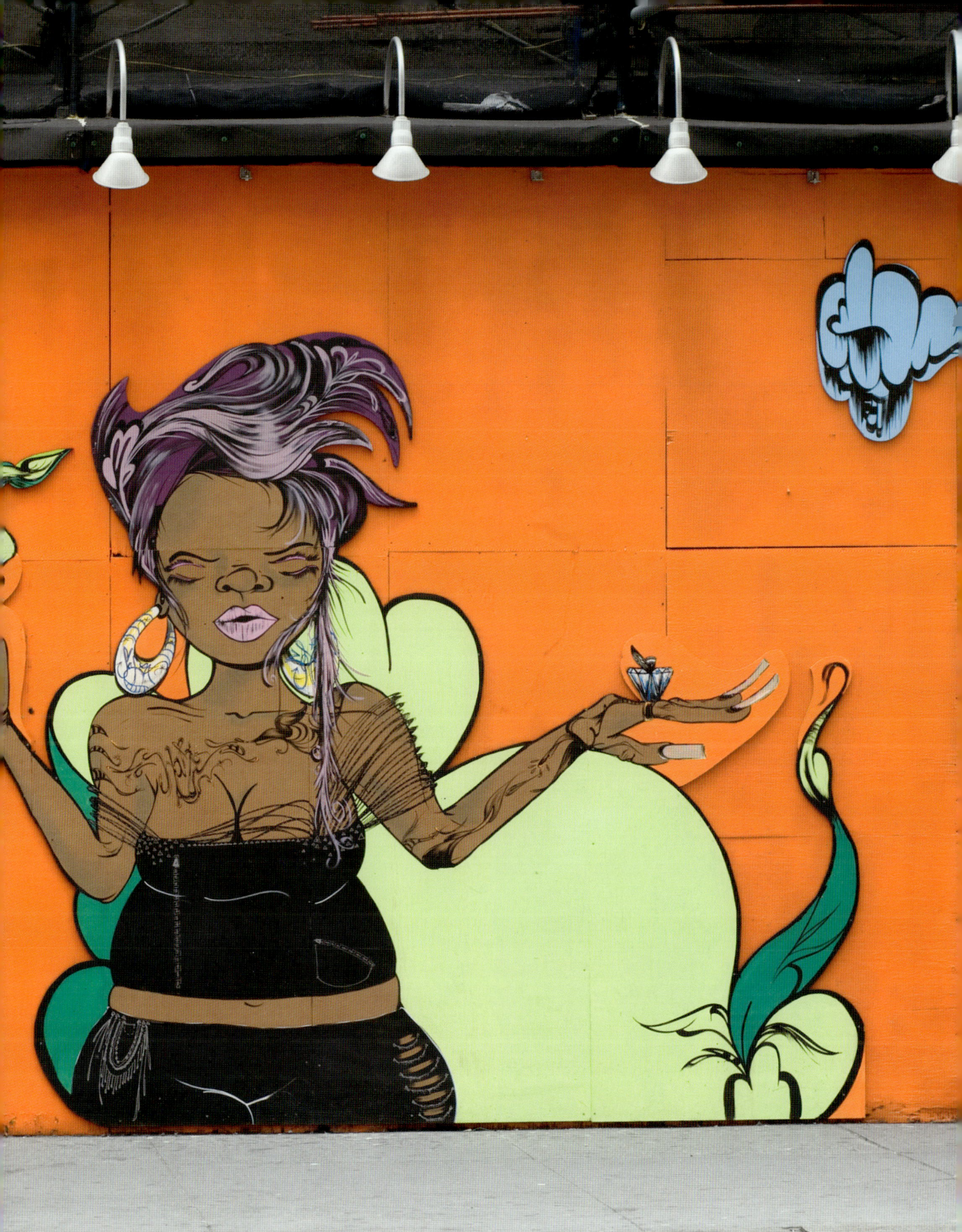

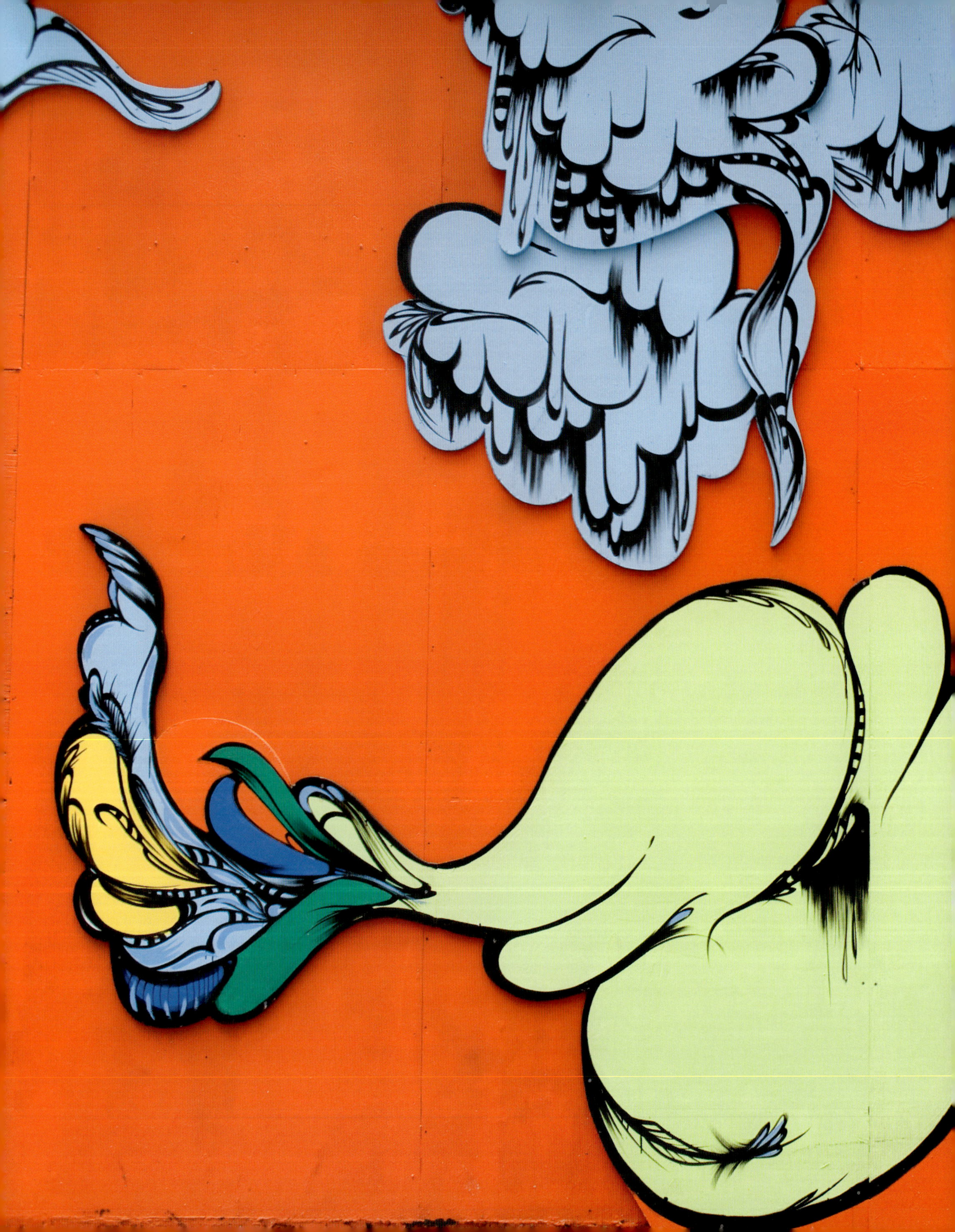

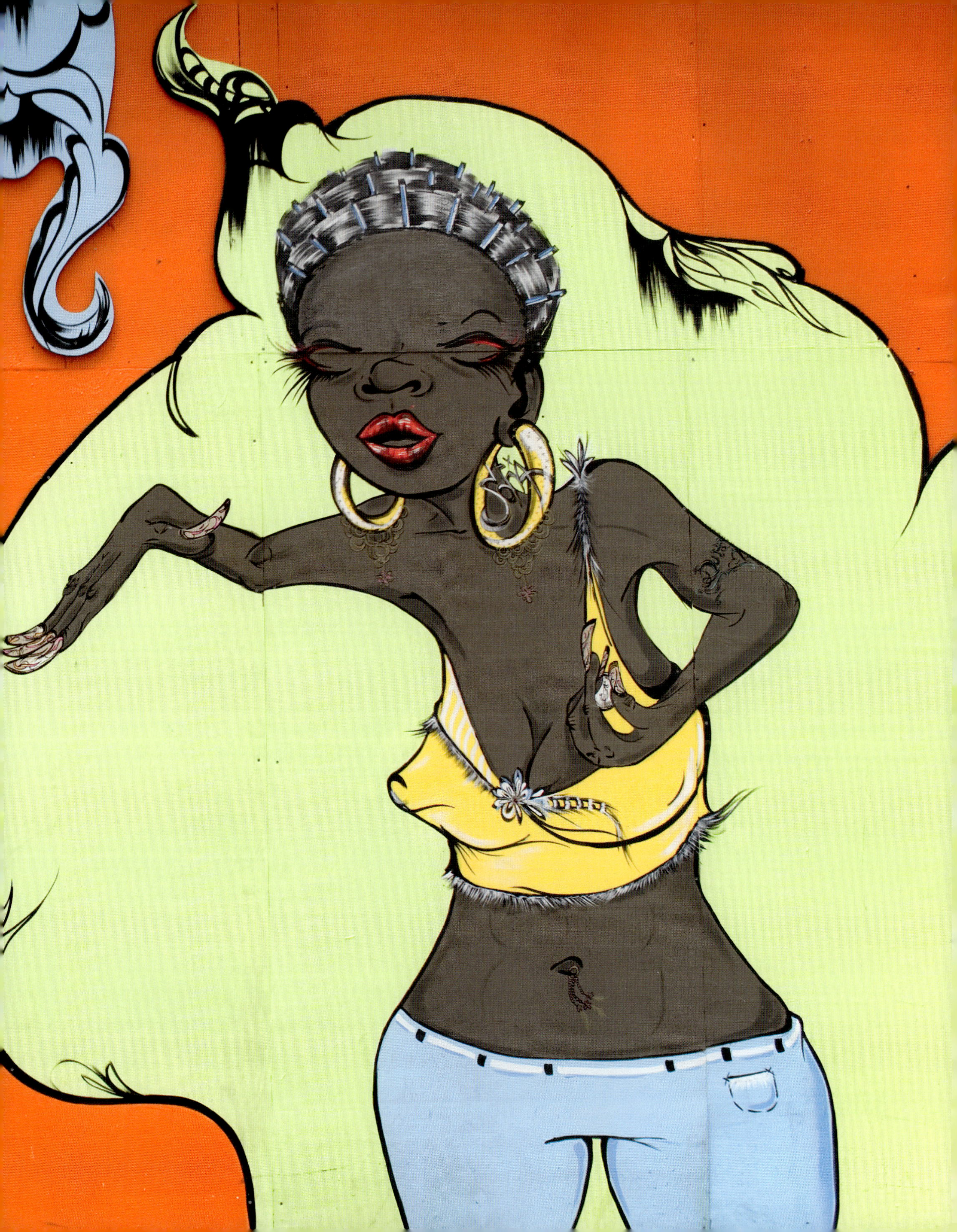

The depiction of women in Maldonado's 42nd Street mural, 2010, offended some who felt the figures were furthering antiquated stereotypes of women of color. Dressed in short skirts, tank tops, and tube tops, with long brightly painted fingernails, big jewelry, and even bigger cleavage, these women are meant to be, in the words of the artist, "brave, strong, and tough women who have to overcome struggles in their daily lives and sometimes impose themselves in a male-dominated world."[17] Critics first aired their complaints on the local Fox affiliate, My Fox New York. Passersby described the women as "ghetto" and "hoodlum." Anthony Herbert, identified as a community advocate, asked, "Why are they not standing here with briefcases and cell phones or even communicating with people to show the professionalism of black and Latino women?" The video subsequently posted on the My Fox New York website drew comments both supporting the artist's vision as well as those who agreed the figures were offensive and unrealistic.

In response, Maldonado posted a reply on the popular news website, The Huffington Post, in which she argued that respectability and success should not be linked to a particular dress code.

> As a Caribbean woman I feel these images have opened a discussion about how people identify with and visualize the women that dress like this in our communities. The protestors have called these characters degrading names such as: "cheap hoes," "prostitutes," "going back to the past," "section 8". . . etc. Respect should not be linked to a dress code. Who has made us believe that this way of dressing is cheap? Or negative? Why do women like this, which exist in our society, offend people? Can't these women in our society be smart, hard-working individuals? Who has imposed the "correct" image through the years? Isn't there room in art for them too?

Those familiar with her work would instantly recognize her style in the mural's figures—the fluidity of line, which comes directly from graffiti, as well as the overtly, even perhaps aggressively, confrontational women.

The Latino and Caribbean communities largely embraced the 42nd Street mural (as well as other projects such as her "Real Art Ways" public art project in Hartford, Connecticut); most of the opposition came from the African American community. Thus the mural seems to have provoked concerns which have surrounded hip-hop from its beginning, namely that the lyrics, fashions, and videos associated with hip-hop culture furthered detrimental stereotyping of the African American (and Latino) communities as violent, over-sexed, and criminal. That this imagery would provoke such outrage in 2010 points to the fact that, regardless of its ubiquity and seeming acceptance, hip-hop continues to inhabit a tenuous position both within the communities from which it came (African American, Caribbean, and Latino), as well as the communities to which it has been "exported" (namely, white suburban America).

As a product of a world that has always known hip-hop, it is of little surprise that Maldonado, who tends towards subject matter firmly situated within what she deems a "post-feminist" paradigm, would choose as the centerpiece for her latest New York gallery exhibition five portraits of hip-hop celebrity. Collectively known as *Concrete Jungle Divas*, Beyoncé, Lady GaGa, Rihanna, J-Lo, and M.I.A. are rendered life-sized with Maldanado's characteristic calligraphic line in vivid tones of pinks, blues, purples, and greens all set off with a bling-bling shimmer of gold dust worked into the acrylic and urethane. The high-gloss gold backgrounds are meant to recall the bamboo shoot earrings sold on Fulton Street in Brooklyn, a reference to Maldonado's deep interest in the diverse neighborhoods of Manhattan.

In discussing why she chose each of these women, she asserts in the exhibition's press release that each are, "icons of the multi-faceted female

**SOFIA MALDONADO**
*Concrete Jungle Divas*, 2010
Gold dust, acrylic paint, urethane
36 x 84 inches each
Courtesy of Magnan Metz Gallery, New York
(detail following pages)

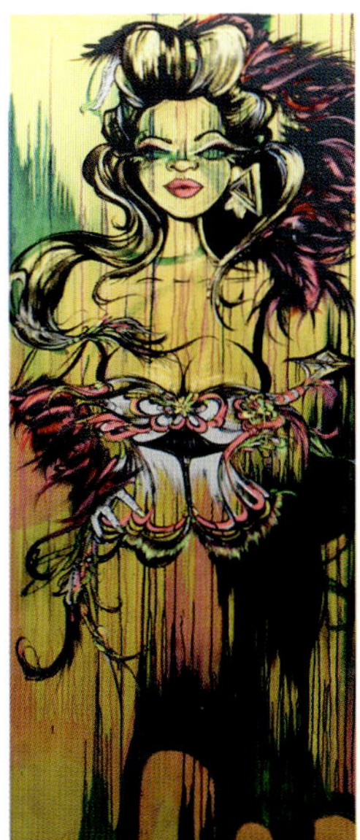
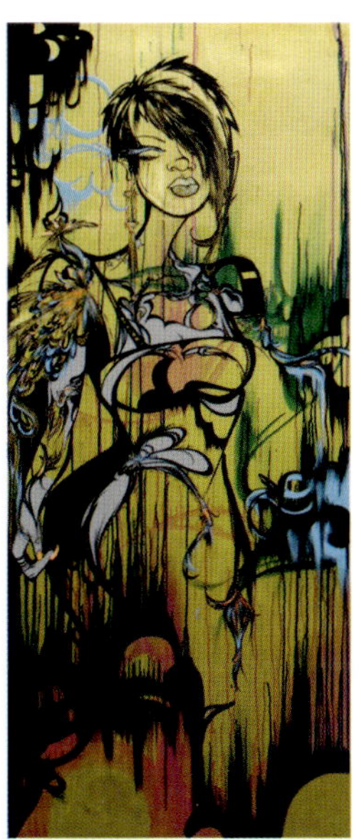
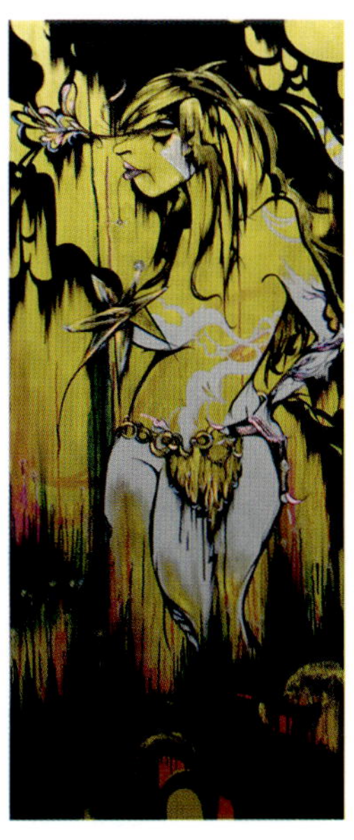
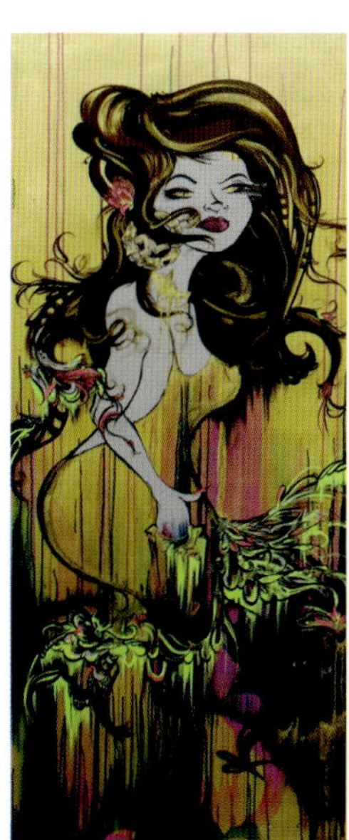
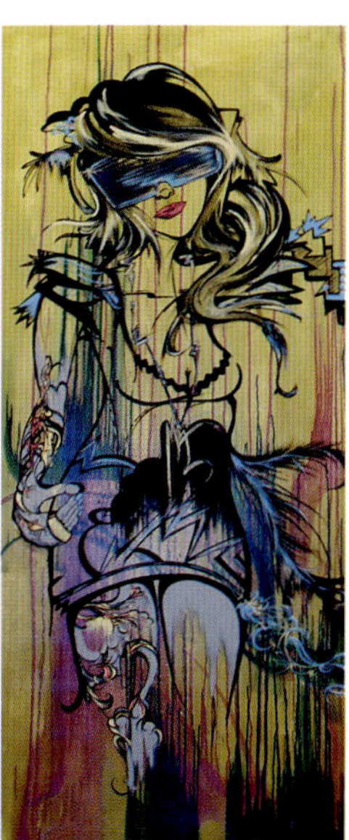

**SOFIA MALDONADO**
Beyoncé from *Concrete Jungle Divas*, 2010
36 x 84 inches
Courtesy of Magnan Metz Gallery, New York

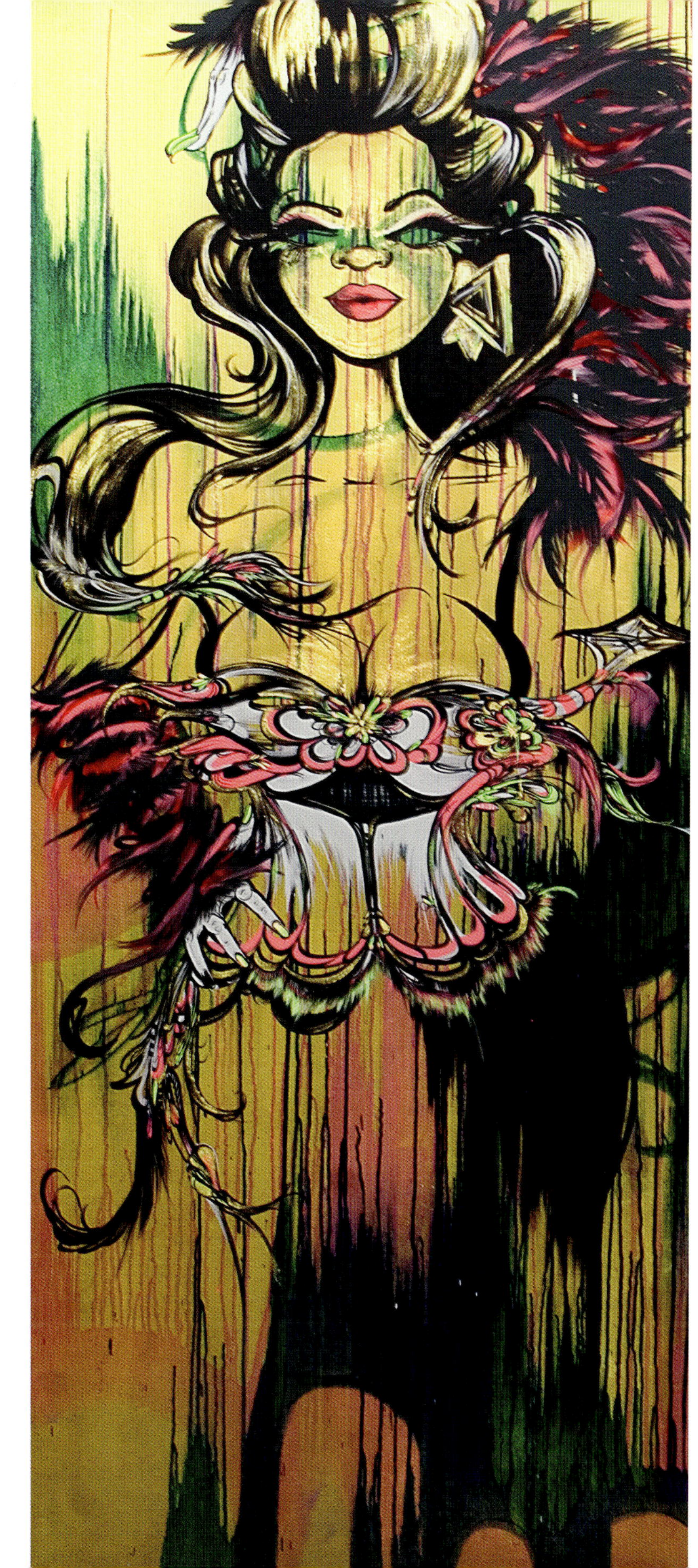

**SOFIA MALDONADO**
Rihanna from *Concrete Jungle Divas*, 2010
36 x 84 inches
Courtesy of Magnan Metz Gallery, New York

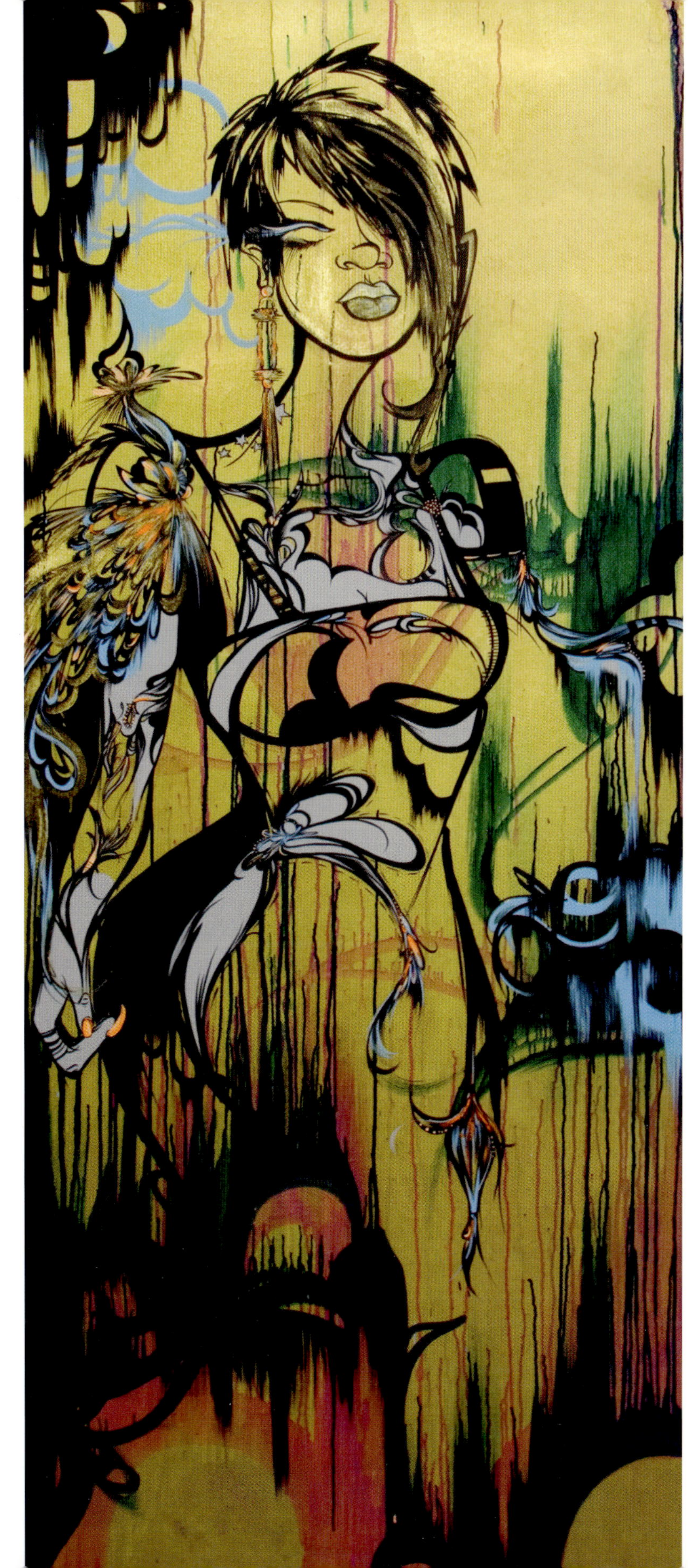

**SOFIA MALDONADO**
Lady GaGa from *Concrete Jungle Divas*, 2010
36 x 84 inches
Courtesy of Magnan Metz Gallery, New York

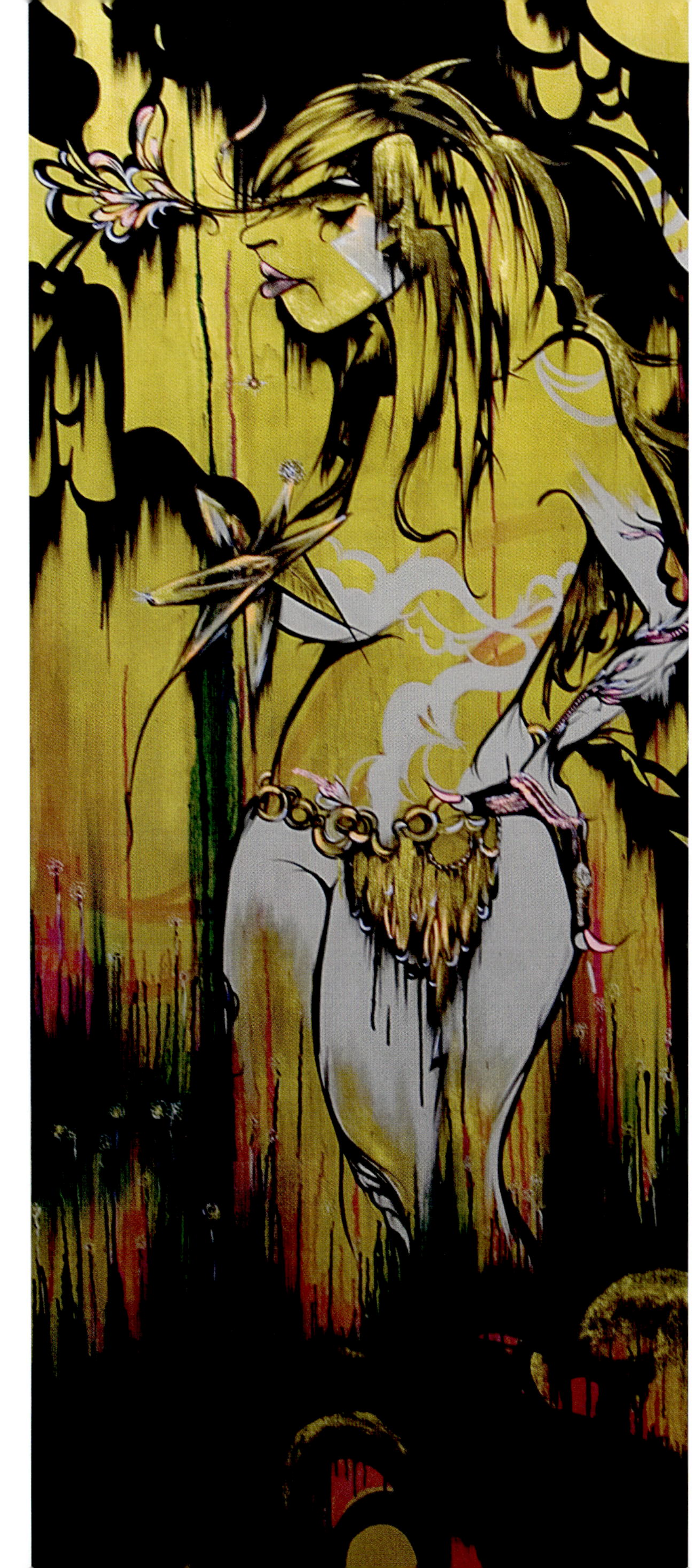

**SOFIA MALDONADO**
J-Lo from *Concrete Jungle Divas*, 2010
36 x 84 inches
Courtesy of Magnan Metz Gallery, New York

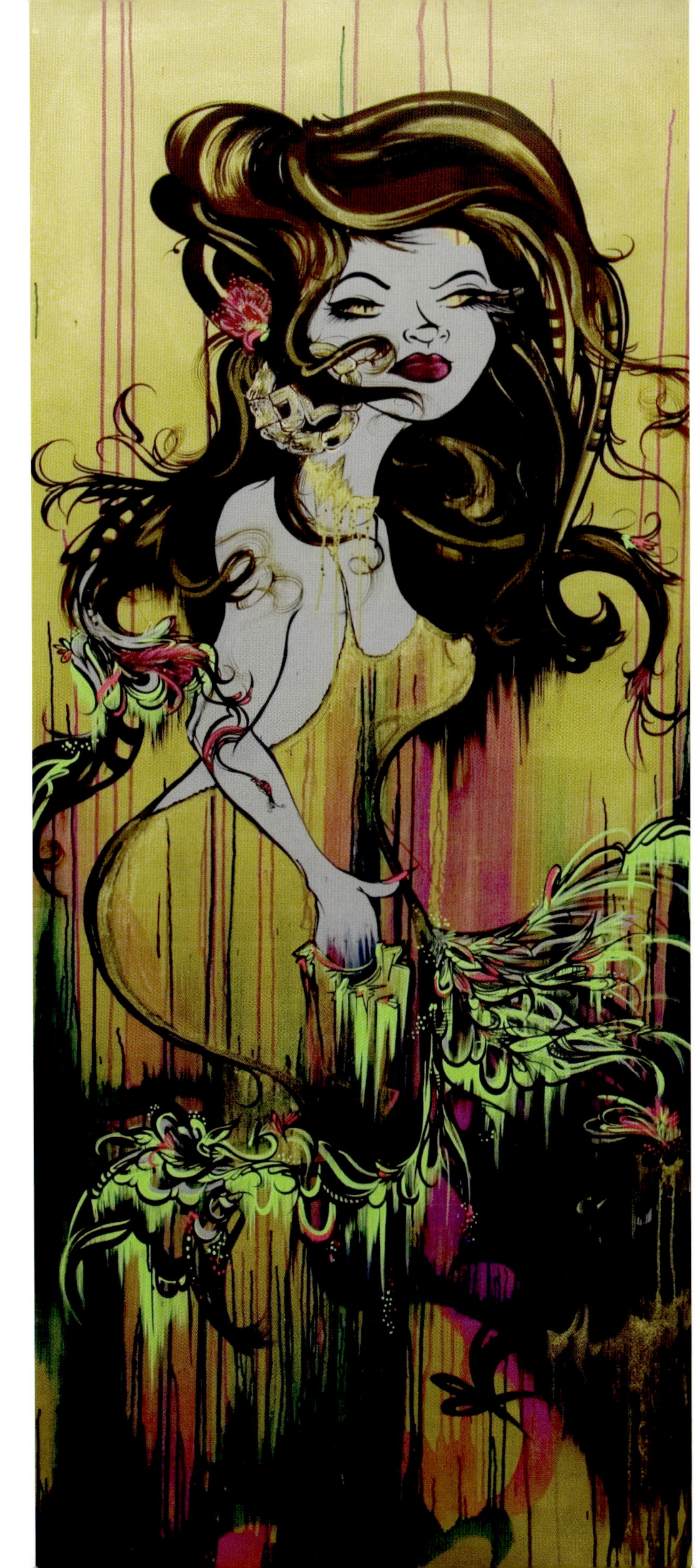

**SOFIA MALDONADO**
M.I.A. from *Concrete Jungle Divas*, 2010
36 x 84 inches
Courtesy of Magnan Metz Gallery, New York

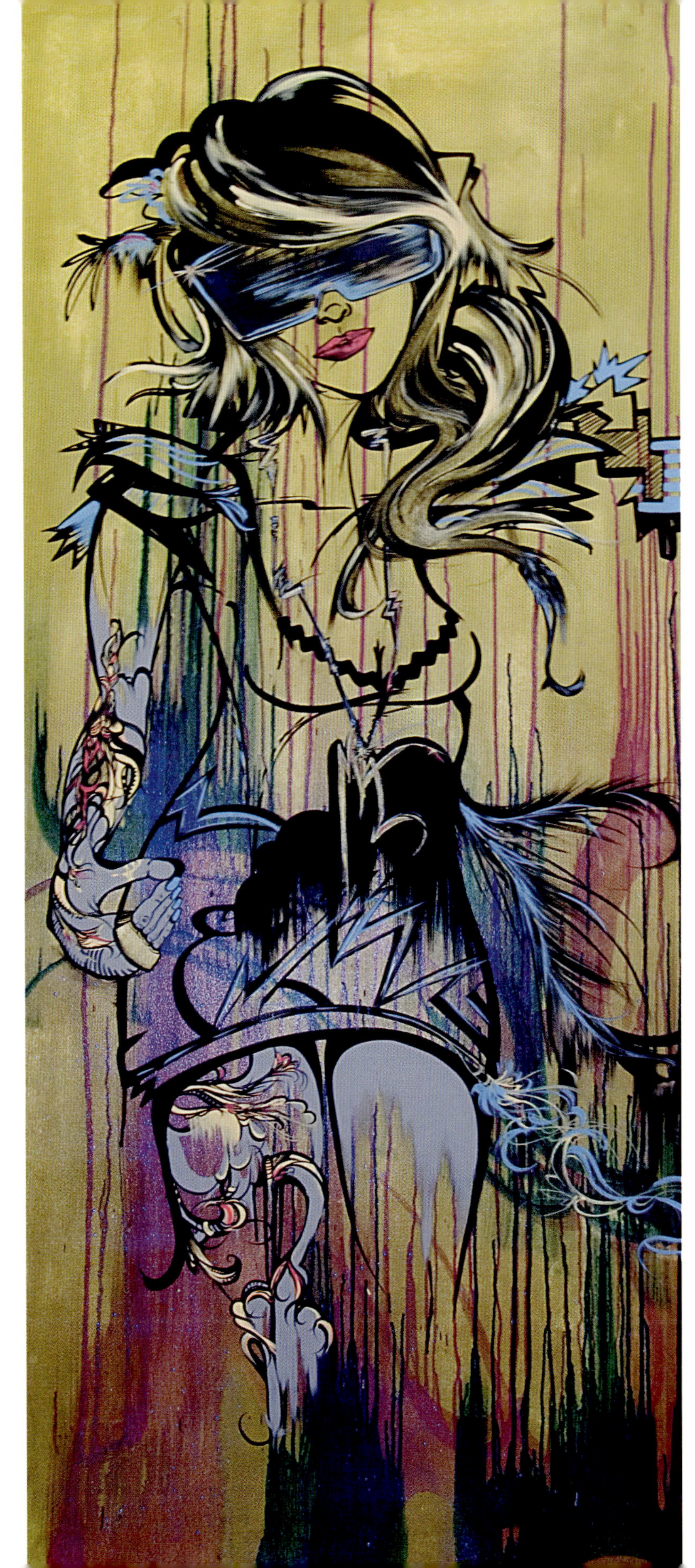

identity: provocateur, sex symbol, workaholic, artist, fashionista." Each of the divas is, again, presented with a frank sexuality for which they neither apologize nor seek to hide and, through their provocative and revealing fashions, could elicit the same types of negative reactions as the 42nd Street mural. However, they did not. Arguably celebrities in our culture are allowed to easily transgress societal expectations whereas the "everyday" women Maldonado sought to celebrate in her 42nd Street mural are denied the distance of the pedestal on which celebrity resides.

Approaching female power from a space that is simultaneously historical and contemporary, Mickalene Thomas samples traditional paradigms, layering them with today's notions of power and respect. Citing the canon of modernist male "genius" (Henri Matisse, Edouard Manet, Paul Gauguin) as sources of inspiration, Thomas has transformed one of the dominant images of female sexuality within modernism, the odalisque, into a statement of frank, sexually charged, female power. *Naughty Girls (Need Love Too)*, 2009, presents all of the elements that have catapulted Thomas to the forefront of contemporary art in America. Composed of intricate interplays of pattern and color, inspired by the patterning in the work of African photographers Malick Sidibé and Seydou Keïta, a sumptuous interior confronts the viewer, calling to mind both the luxurious private spaces of Western Orientalist fantasy as well as the funky 1970s interiors Thomas credits for the retro feel her paintings often evoke.

The subject of *Naughty Girls (Need Love Too)*, herself a cacophony of pattern, arches her back in the pose long associated with ecstasy within the Western artistic canon. Yet, while it is undeniable that this woman has been offered up for the scopophilic gaze of the viewer, she is an active, rather than the traditionally passive, participant in this power play. Looking directly out of the panel, sparkle pink lips parted, white teeth showing, this "odalisque," far from being the submissive object of sexual release, gives every indication that she enjoys the attention of the viewer and will equally revel in the ensuing ecstasy foreshadowed in her pose.

The subversion of the male gaze has, of course, been much explored in feminist art and critique. However, the fact that Mickalene Thomas is openly gay further layers subversive strata within the readings given her paintings. Thomas is thus able to straddle the space of the historic paradigm of male artist/female model as one who embodies the convergence of the desirer and the desired. And because Thomas's female models are African American, she also broaches the historical phenomenon, particularly potent within modernist studies, of the fetishization of black skin.[18] As a reservoir of Western European fantasies of primal desire (a prime example being the reception of Josephine Baker's tightly constructed persona in 1920s Paris), one could criticize Thomas's works, which not only employ slick enamels for the fashioning of the skin, but, most famously, are studded with thousands of rhinestones thus calling attention to the already conspicuous surface as well as reinforcing the "object-ness" of the painting and, therefore, the subject. Thomas, however, argues against any notion that her portraits further fetishize black skin. She states, "As the artist, I use surface-level clues as indicators of what lies beneath the surface of the individual."[19] The rhinestones are to remind the viewer of the artifice of the make-up, fashions, and hairstyles that comprise the initial photo shoot, and in Thomas's estimation, reinforce both the work's surface and the basic tension in portraiture.

Thomas's richly encrusted surfaces also recall the depictions of otherworldliness by Byzantine and Early Renaissance masters. Studding their gold-ground images of heavenly hosts with colored glass to replicate jewels, employing techniques such as *pastiglia* (the application of a thick paste to imitate metalwork), and the use of the most costly materials available, namely gold leaf and lapis lazuli, proto-Renaissance artists created expensive objects of concrete wealth. These objects were the embodiment of the divine status of the Madonnas and Infant Christs they portrayed. In a similar way, Mickalene Thomas's paintings raise up her subjects through the actual luxuriousness of the object itself. These contemporary women depicted are thus recast not only as exotic women in control of their sexual power, but also as women touched by, or the embodiment of, the divine.

**MICKALENE THOMAS**
*Naughty Girls (Need Love Too)*, 2009
Rhinestone, acrylic, and enamel on panel
96 x 120 x 2 inches
Courtesy of the artist and Lehmann Maupin Gallery, New York
(detail following pages)

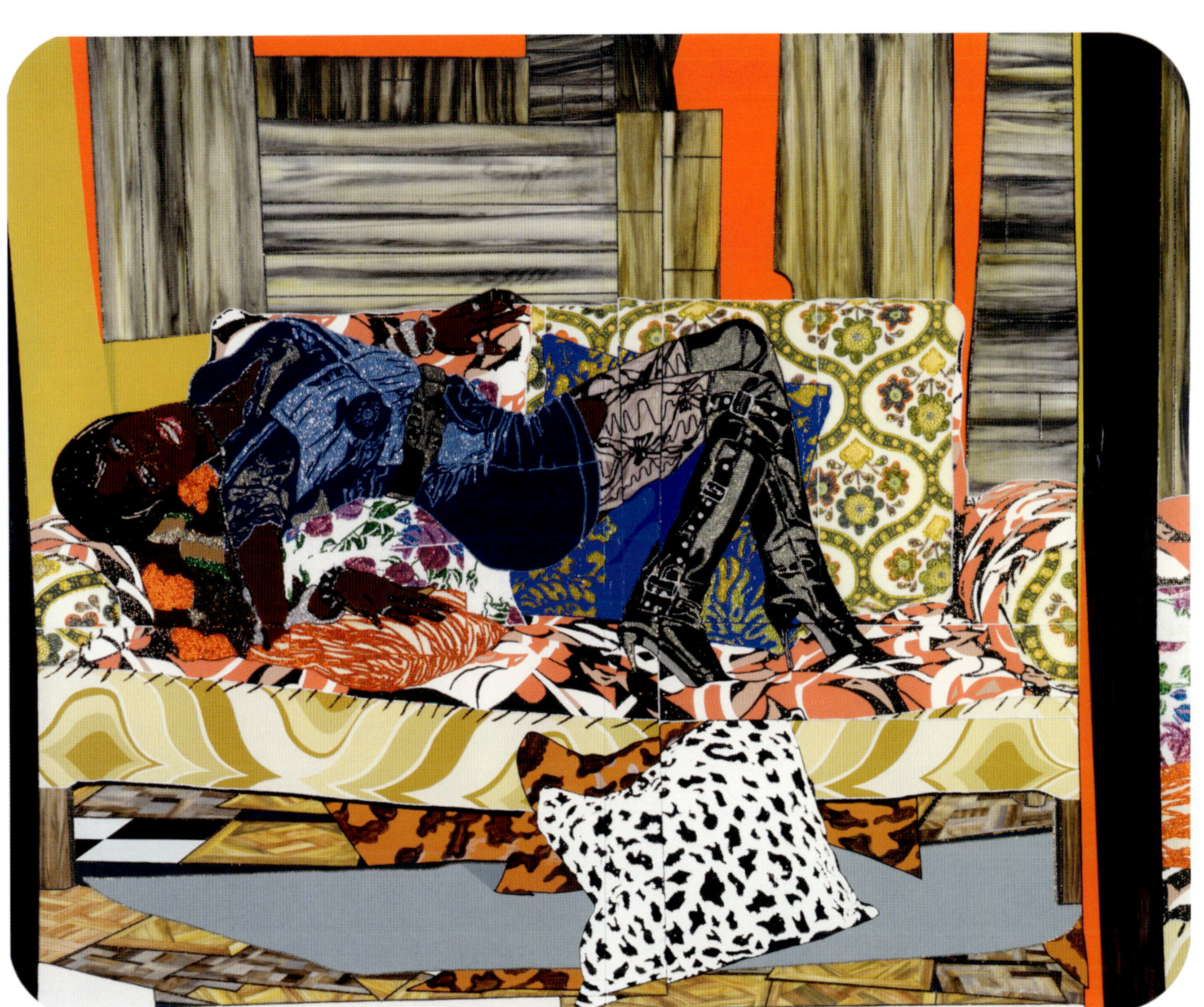

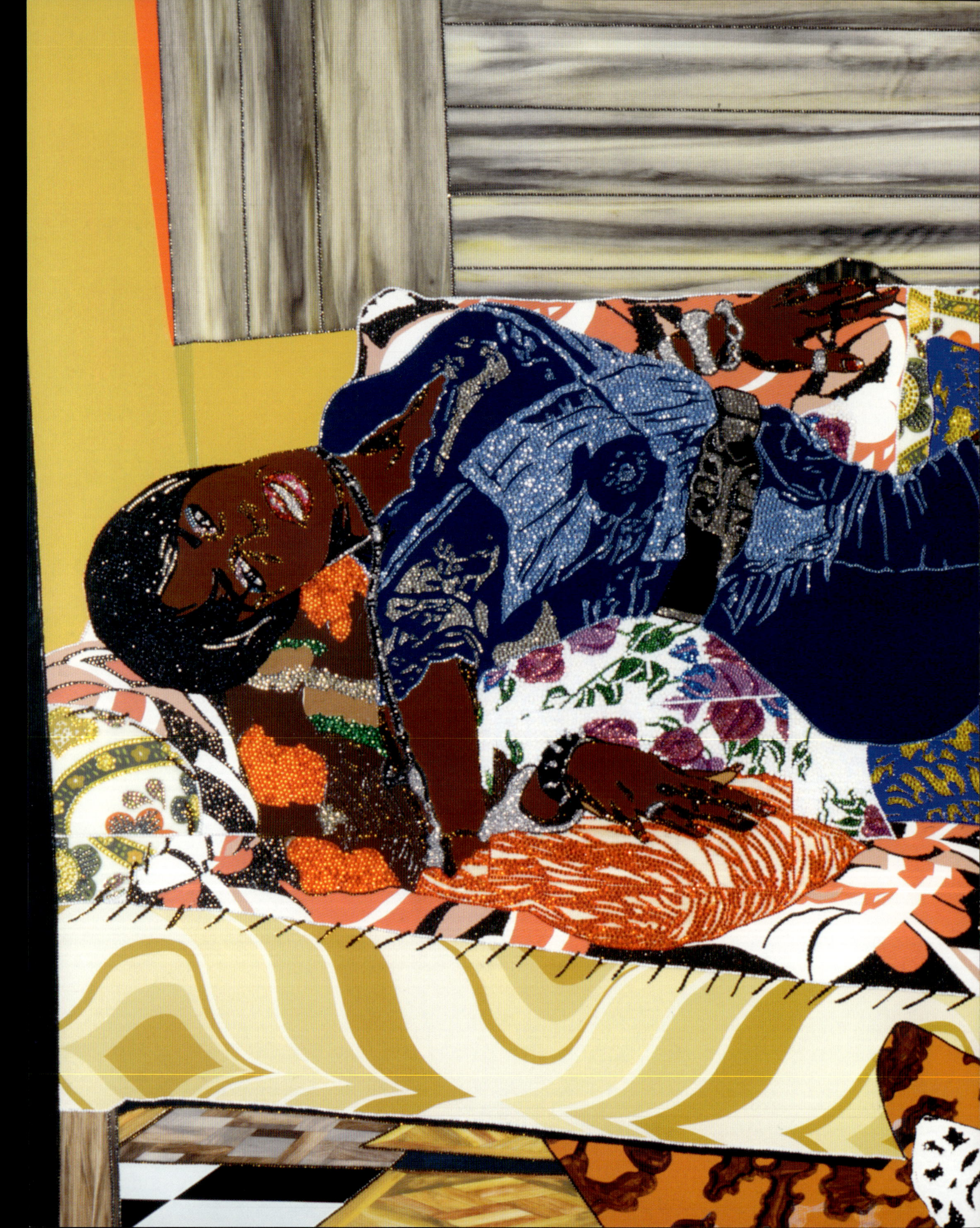

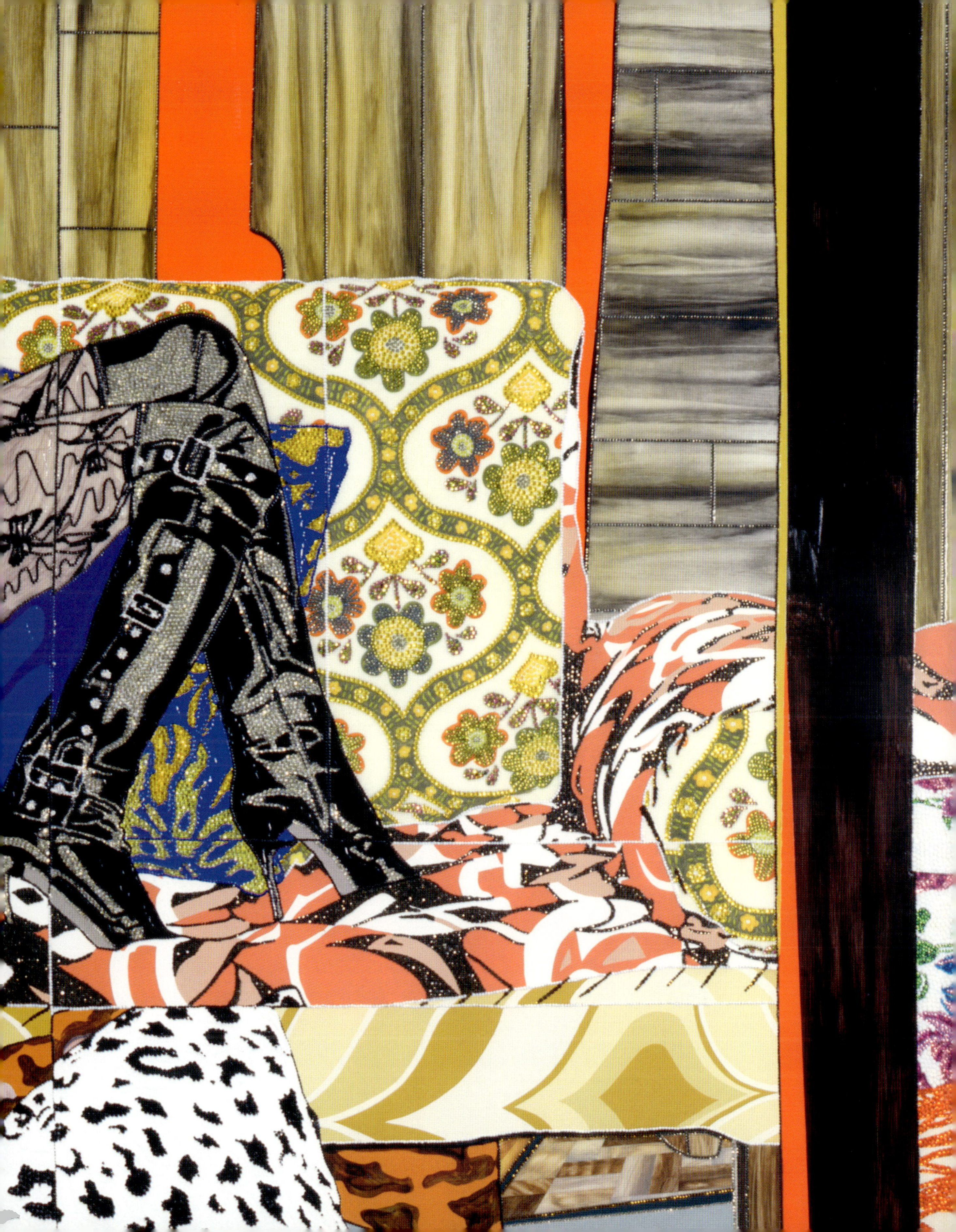

**MICKALENE THOMAS**
*Ain't I a Woman (Sandra)*, 2009
DVD and framed monitor, rhinestones, acrylic, and enamel on panel
Diptych: 36 x 28 inches (painting);
18 x 24 x 5⅜16 inches (framed monitor)
Edition 2 of 3, 2 AP
Courtesy of the artist and Lehmann Maupin Gallery, New York

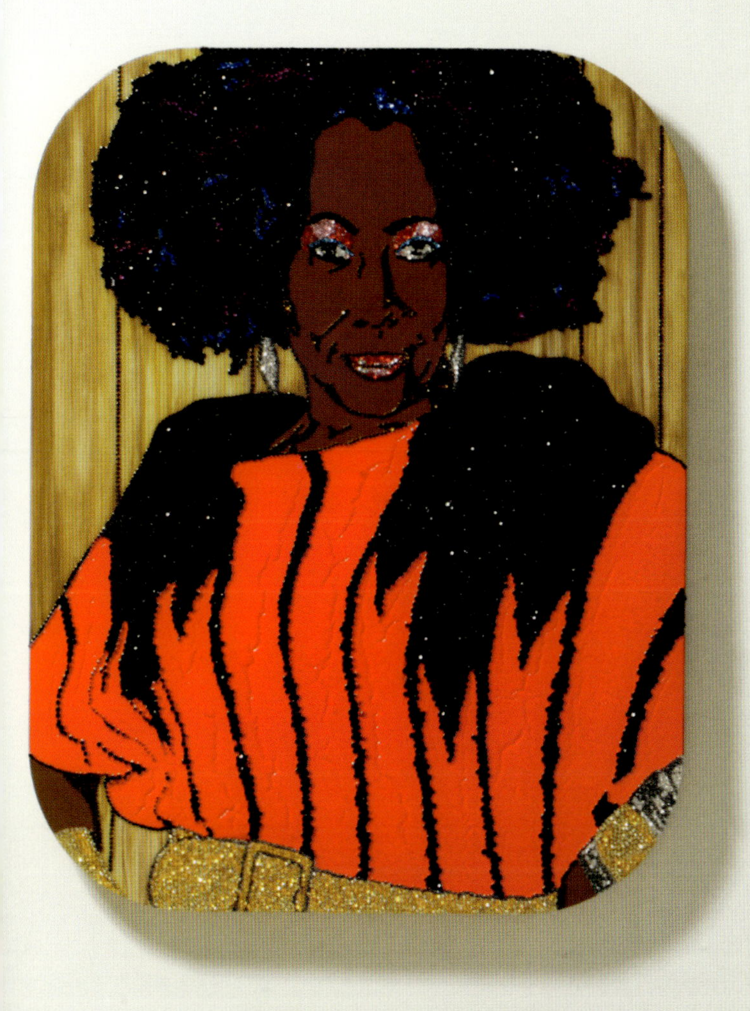

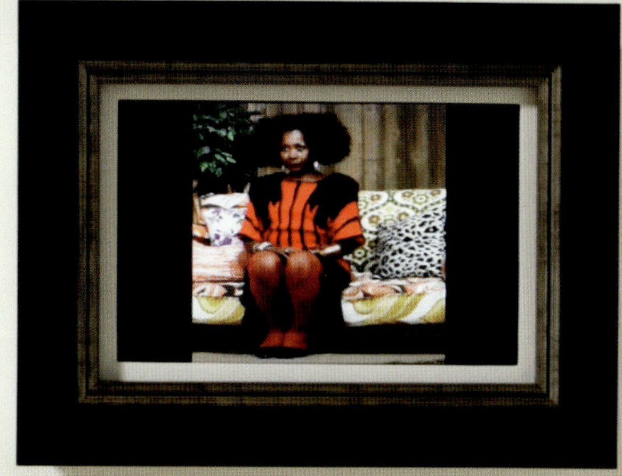

Recently, Thomas has taken to displaying aspects of the process she uses to arrive at the final, often monumental, paintings. In the diptych *Ain't I a Woman (Sandra)*, 2009, Thomas pairs one of her characteristically sequined portraits—this one of her favorite model, her mother—with a video showing the photo shoot undertaken as part of the initial process leading to the painting. Crossing the lines between theater, fashion, and fine art, Thomas uses the photography sessions as a basis—a sketch—for the final work. By exhibiting the videos, she offers the viewer entrée into the private world of the artist and model illustrating the great lengths she takes to make the models first comfortable and then redolent with the emotional tone she wishes them to project. However, Thomas only allows the viewer so far in to the private aspect of this process.

Rather than allowing the intimate conversation between artist and model to be replayed for public consumption, Eartha Kitt purrs *A Woman Wouldn't Be A Woman* over the action of the video leaving the viewer to question the full content of the recorded experience. The juxtaposition of the title of the series, *Ain't I A Woman* (taken from the former slave and abolitionist Sojurner Truth's famed speech given at the Women's Convention in Akron, Ohio, in 1851), the lyrics of Kitt's song advancing 1950s stereotypes of women's behavior, and the powerfully confident portrait of her mother—certainly capable of being read as a Madonna figure given Thomas's deep visual conversations with art history—perfectly demonstrates the complex navigation of historical and contemporary issues that she deftly weaves in her work.

Mickalene Thomas is certainly not the first to sample motifs from the history of art. Kehinde Wiley came to prominence through his unrepentant updating of the Western, white, canon. In works such as *Raphael The Ecstasy of St. Cecilia*, 2005, from the *Passing/Posing* series, and *Simon George I*, 2006, after a portrait by Hans Holbein, Wiley recasts famous Old Master paintings with the young black men he has noticed on streets throughout the world. Like Thomas, his paintings captivate the viewer with a potent mixture of slickly rendered surfaces, intricate patterning, bold color, and the frank gazes of his subjects. Beyond the hip-hop sampling of history, his men have all of the conspicuous sartorial signifiers of their hip-hop identities: the hoodies, the brand names, the baseball caps, the bling. As with Mickalene Thomas's work, much has been made of the homoeroticism Wiley, who is openly gay, teases out of the original context through the detailed, lovingly rendered depictions of the men, who often come across as modern-day hip-hop dandies. The meticulously rendered, photorealist portraits also operate as signifiers of celebrity even if that celebrity is of the "fifteen-minutes" variety.[20]

As a participant in the rampant celebrity culture that marks so much of American society today, and has long been a component of hip-hop, it is notable that in a conversation with his friend, the singer M.I.A., which appeared in *Interview* magazine (the publication founded by the father of the famous-for-famousness sake culture, Andy Warhol), Wiley decries the lack of surprise at being asked to pose for a monumental painting expressed by some of the men he randomly selected from the streets. Comparing attitudes between the models he had been working with recently in West Africa to those he frequently "street cast" from the Fulton Street Mall in Brooklyn, Wiley laments that with the American men, "there is almost a feeling of entitlement by the public . . . I think part of that is mediated by a very televisual sense of instant celebrity, something that's sort of 'just add water.'"[21]

Though he reverses the usual commissioning process of the portrait by predominately approaching his subjects first, Wiley largely continues a traditional paradigm of portraiture by "ennobling" his subjects. Except for the highest ranks of the nobility, portraiture has always been a genre of aspiration. In street casting his subjects and then re-casting the masterpieces of the canon, often keeping the attributes of power found in the originals, Wiley uses a visual language of power to raise the status of these men who, while their names may be preserved, will most likely lose their larger identities to time.

Through their use of sumptuous and ornate surfaces and references to art history, Mickalene Thomas and Kehinde Wiley both translate the bling-bling aesthetic of hip-hop into high art. The über luxurious lifestyles embodied by hip-hop celebrities and propagated by music videos, print advertising, and the seemingly never dry fountain of reality television has constructed a cult of celebrity within hip-hop for which portraiture is the historic scaffold. In *Bling Pop*, 2006–2007, a portrait of the hip-hop singer and producer Pharrell, the London-based artist and graphic designer Vince Fraser merges the concepts of traditional portraiture and an aesthetic of advertising to produce an image that strips away the pretense of the canonical genre and lays bare the true intention of the portrait—the advertising of a constructed persona in which both the subject and the artist are complicit. In contemporary parlance, portraiture is the forming of a brand. This point is underscored by the layering of the symbol of the bling-bling lifestyle, the BMW, on top of Pharell's torso and further reinforcing the explicitness of the image with the word "BLING" appearing like a tattoo.

**KEHINDE WILEY**
*Passing/Posing (Raphael The Ecstasy of St. Cecilia)*, 2005
Graphite and watercolor on paper
8 x 10 inches
The Jacqueline Bradley and Clarence Otis, Jr. Collection

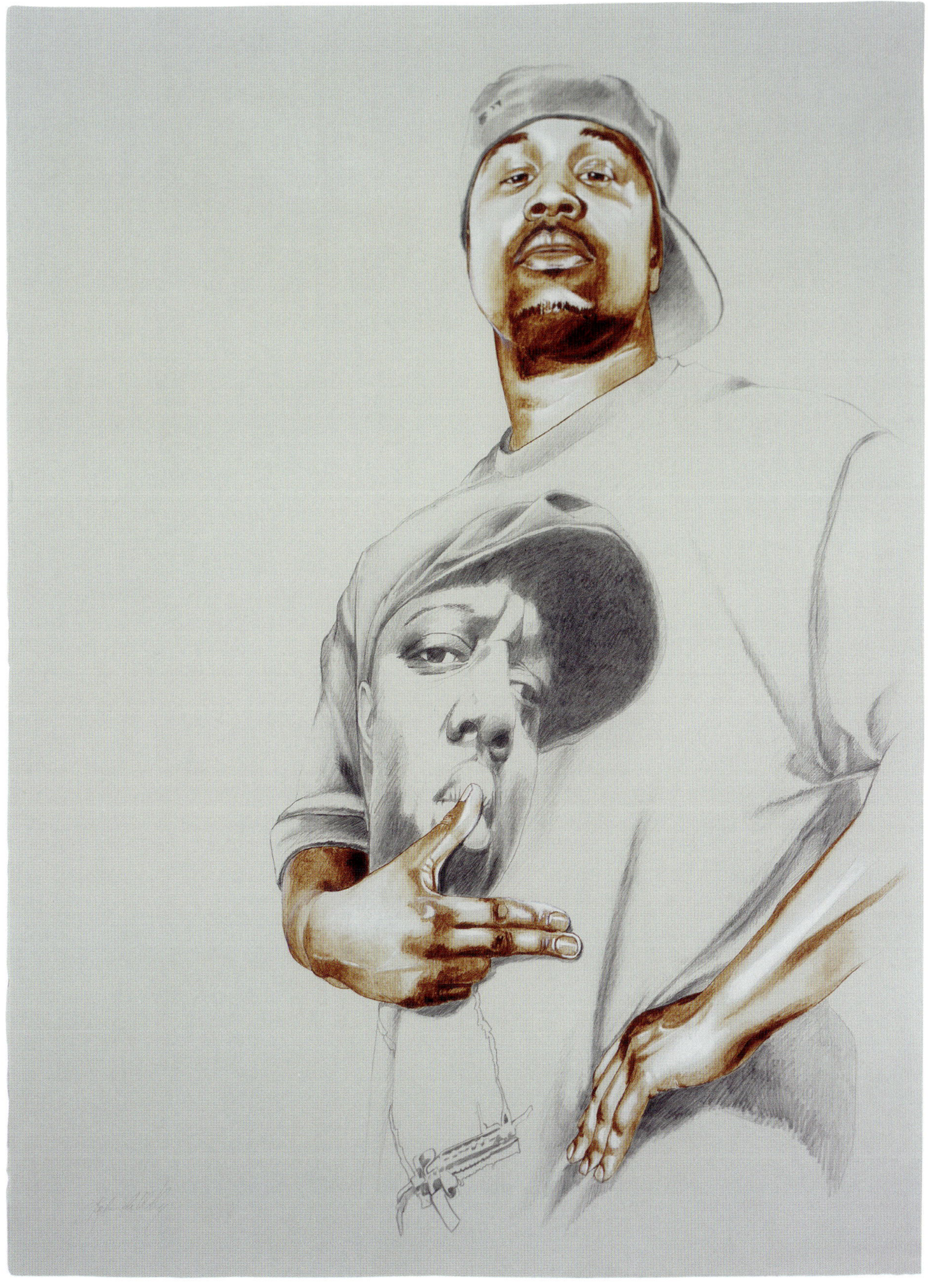

**KEHINDE WILEY**
*Simon George I*, 2006
Oil on canvas
48 x 36 x 2 inches
The Jacqueline Bradley and Clarence Otis, Jr. Collection

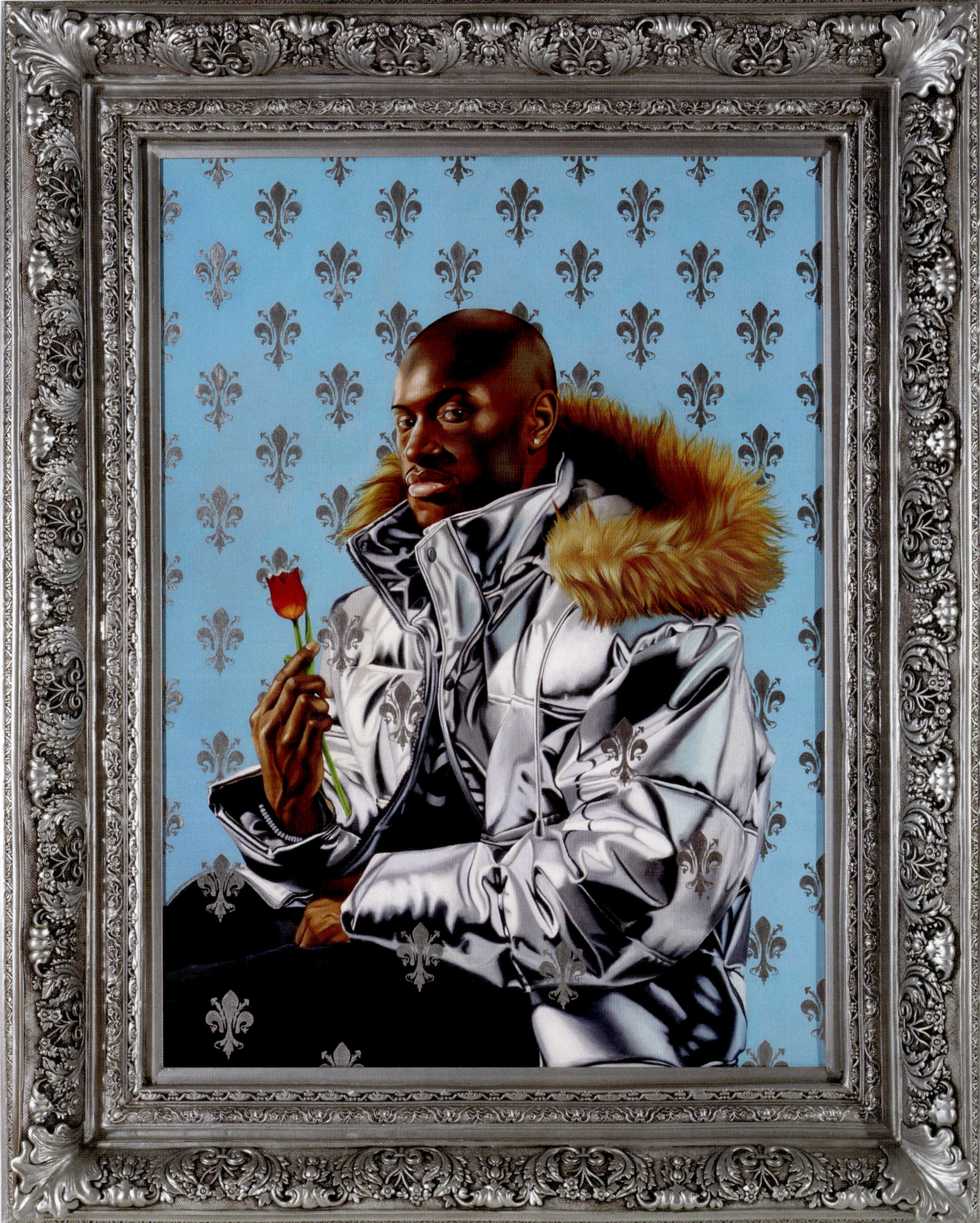

**VINCE FRASER**
*Bling Pop*, 2006–2007
Digital print
Dimensions variable
Courtesy of the artist
(detail following pages)

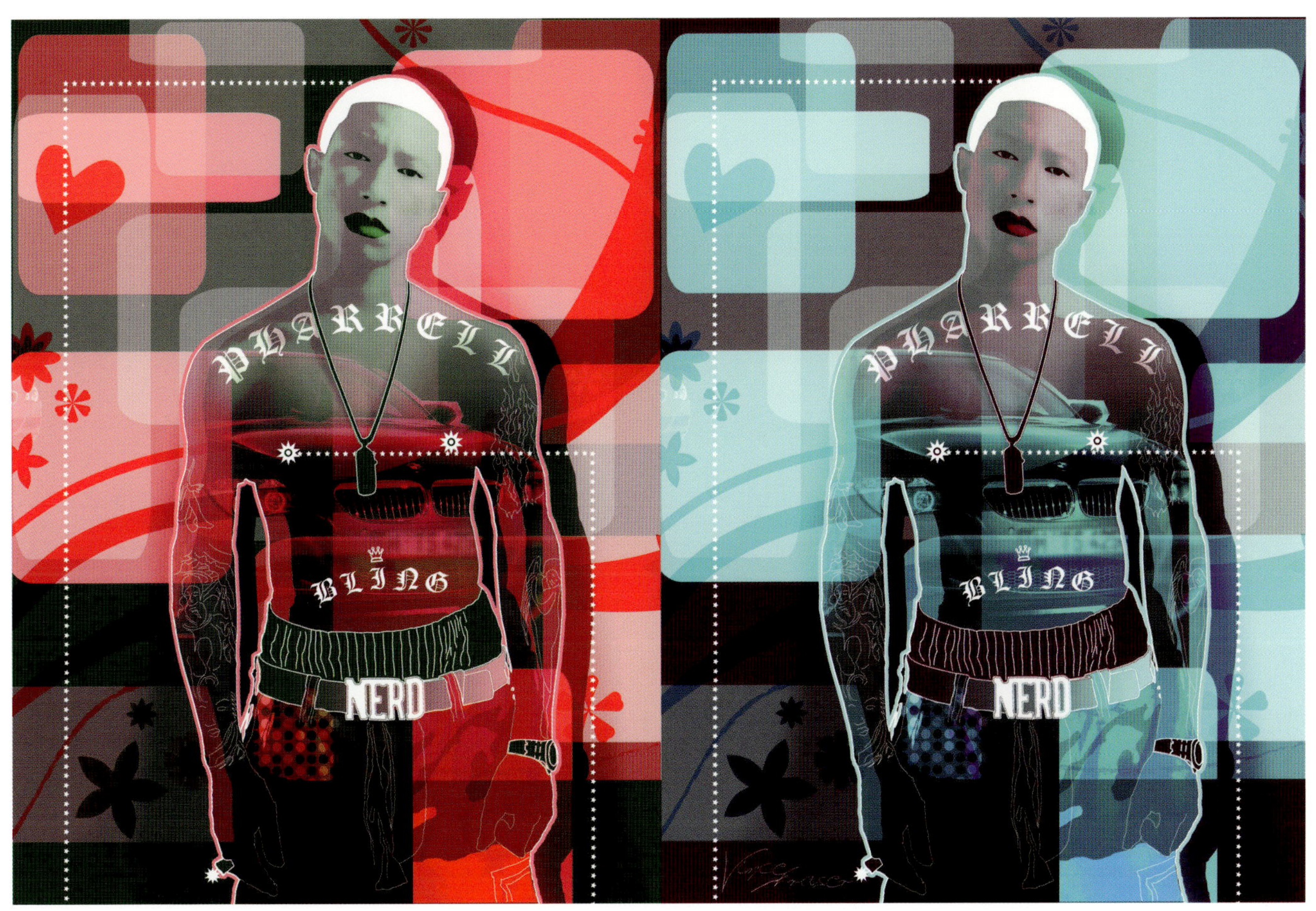
PHARRELL
BLING
NERD
PHARRELL
BLING
NERD

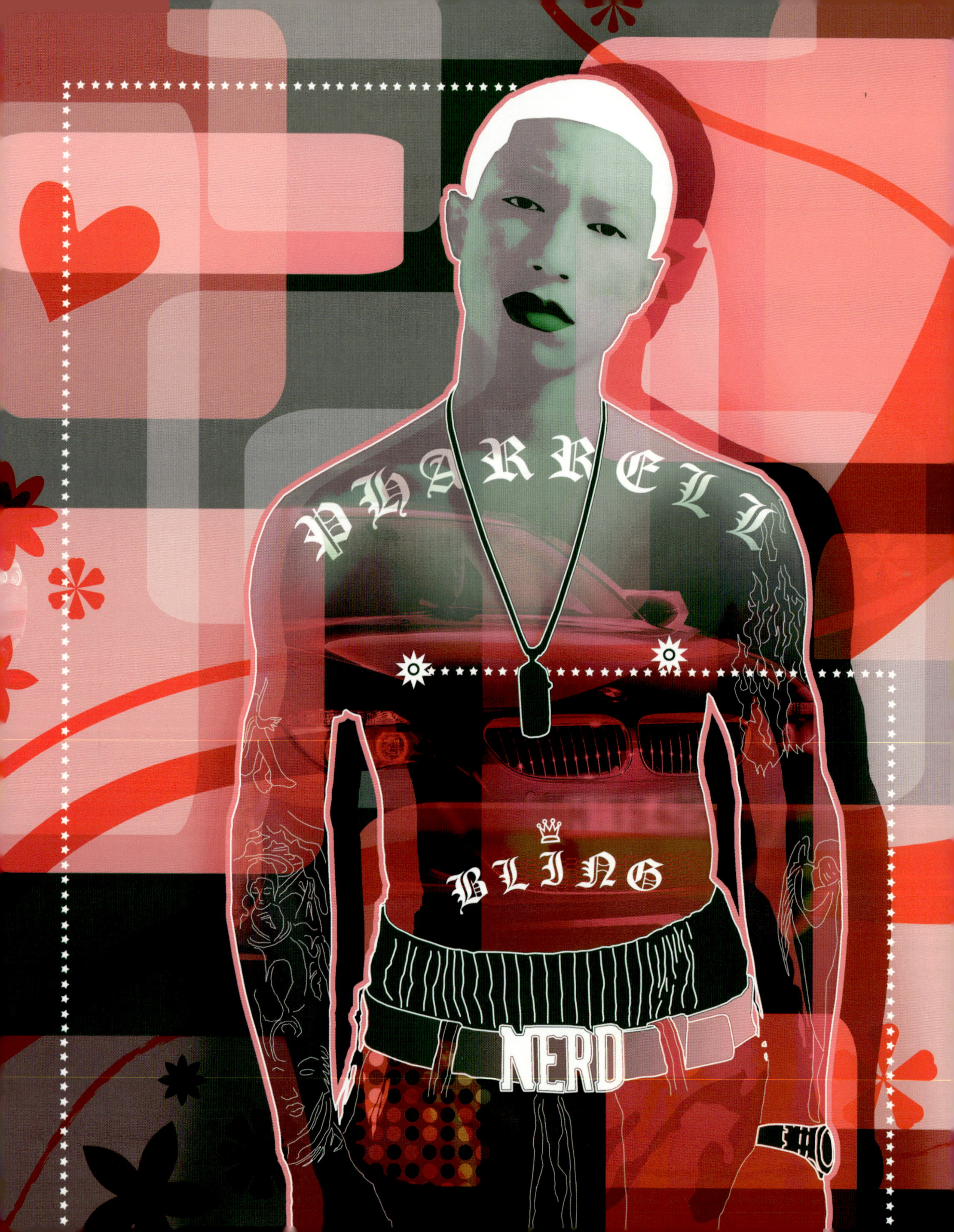
PHARRELL
BLING
NERD

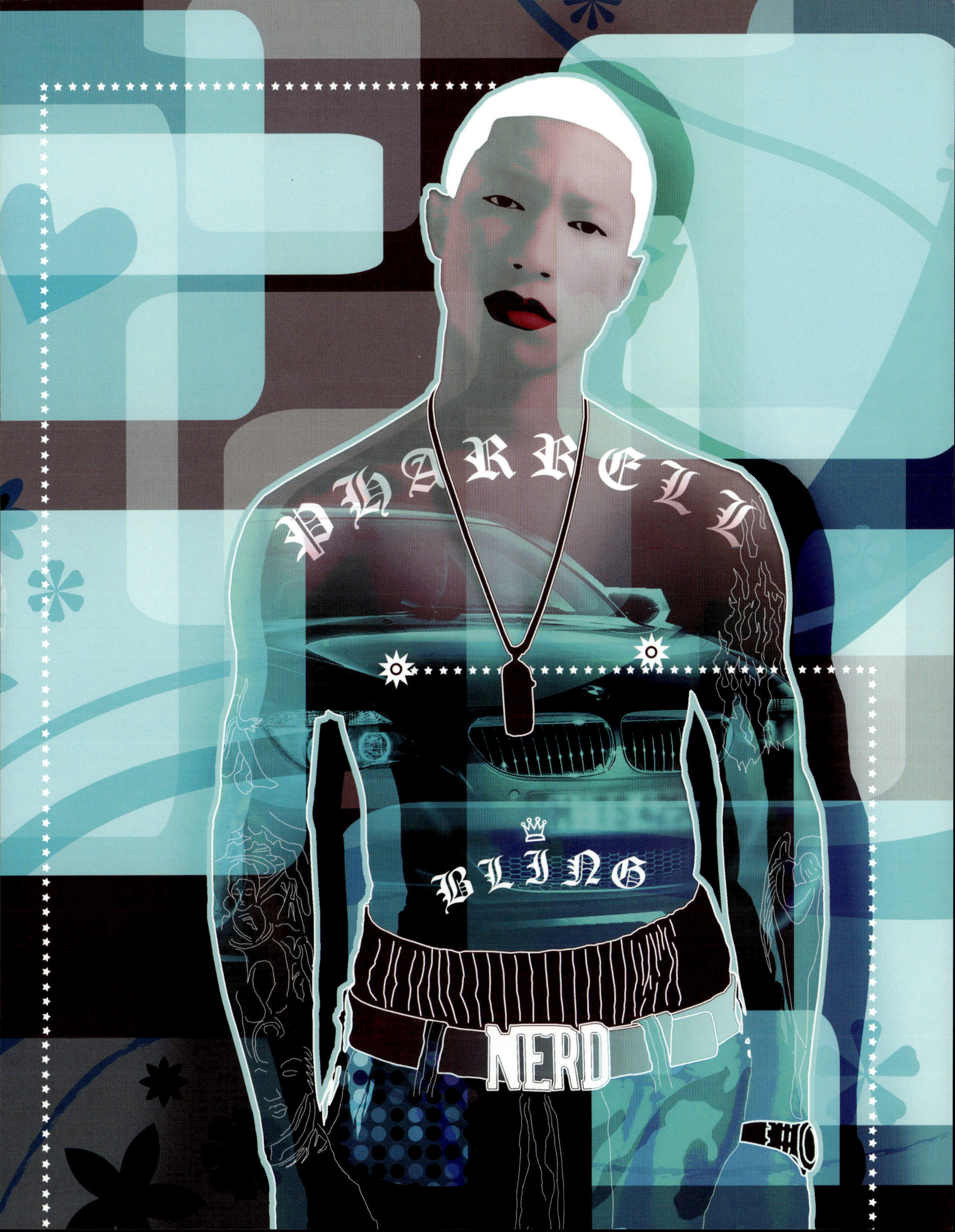
PHARRELL
BLING
NERD

**VINCE FRASER**
*Work & Play*, 2009
Digital print
Dimensions variable
Courtesy of the artist
(detail following pages)

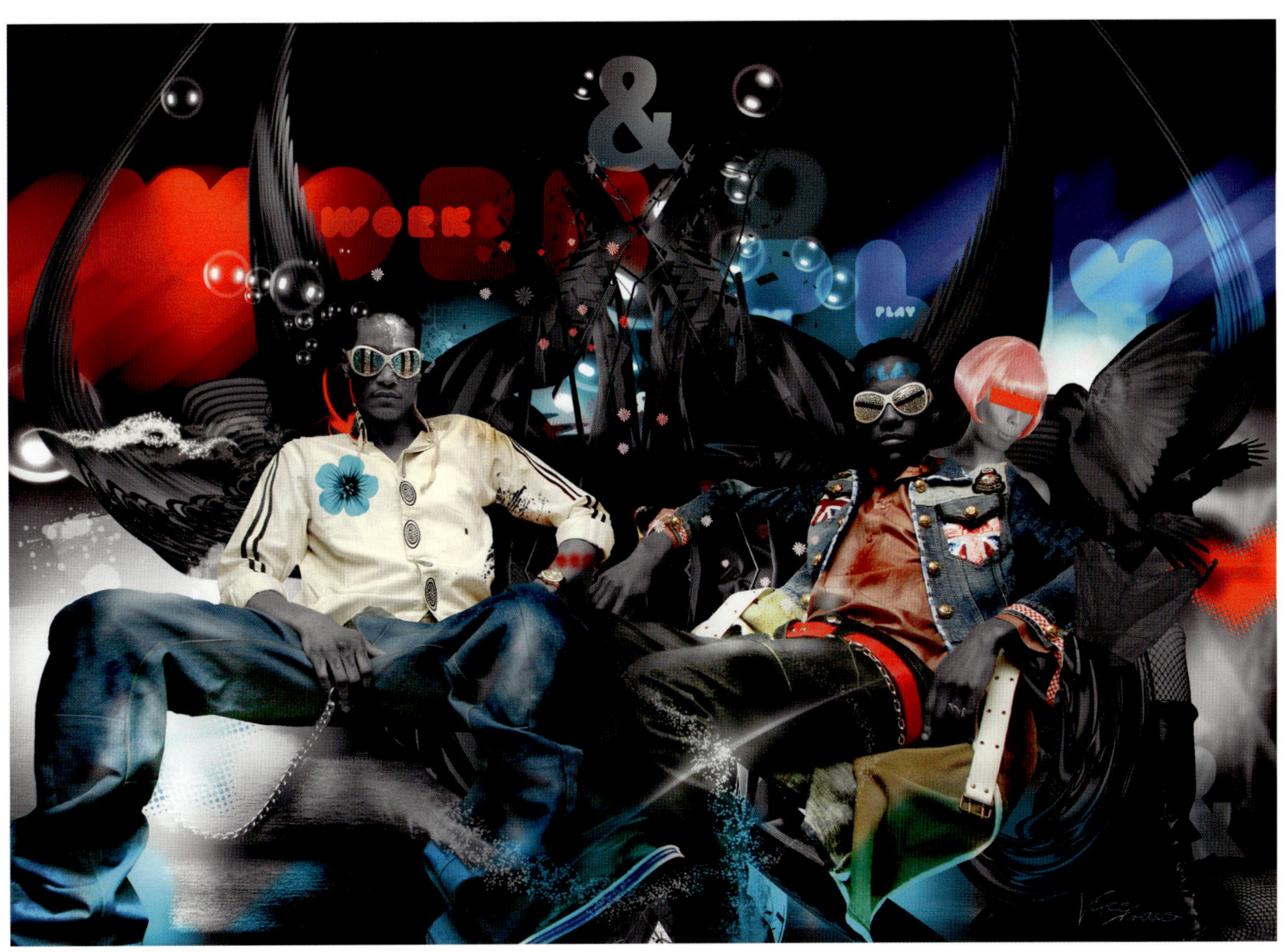
&
WORK
PLAY

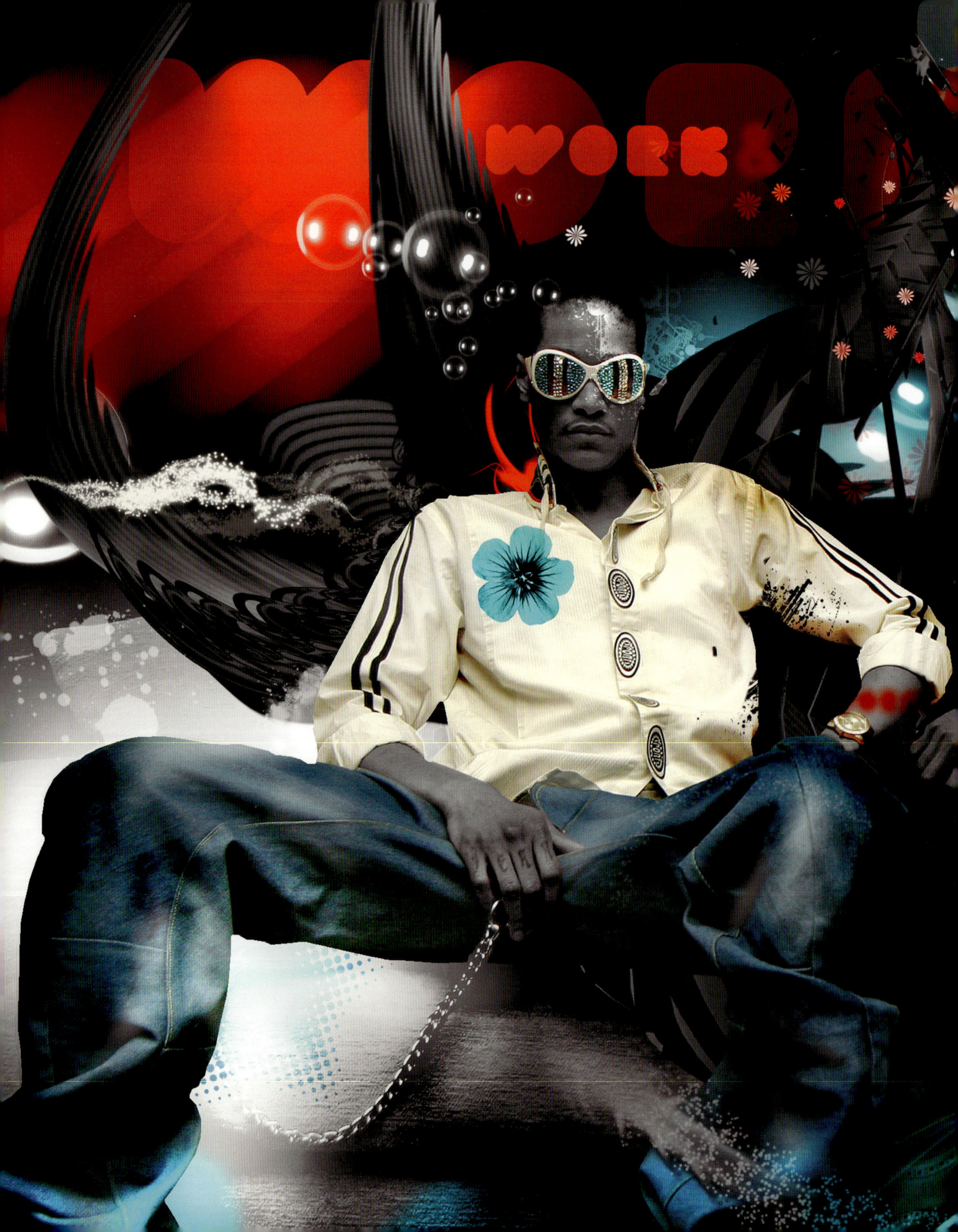
WORK

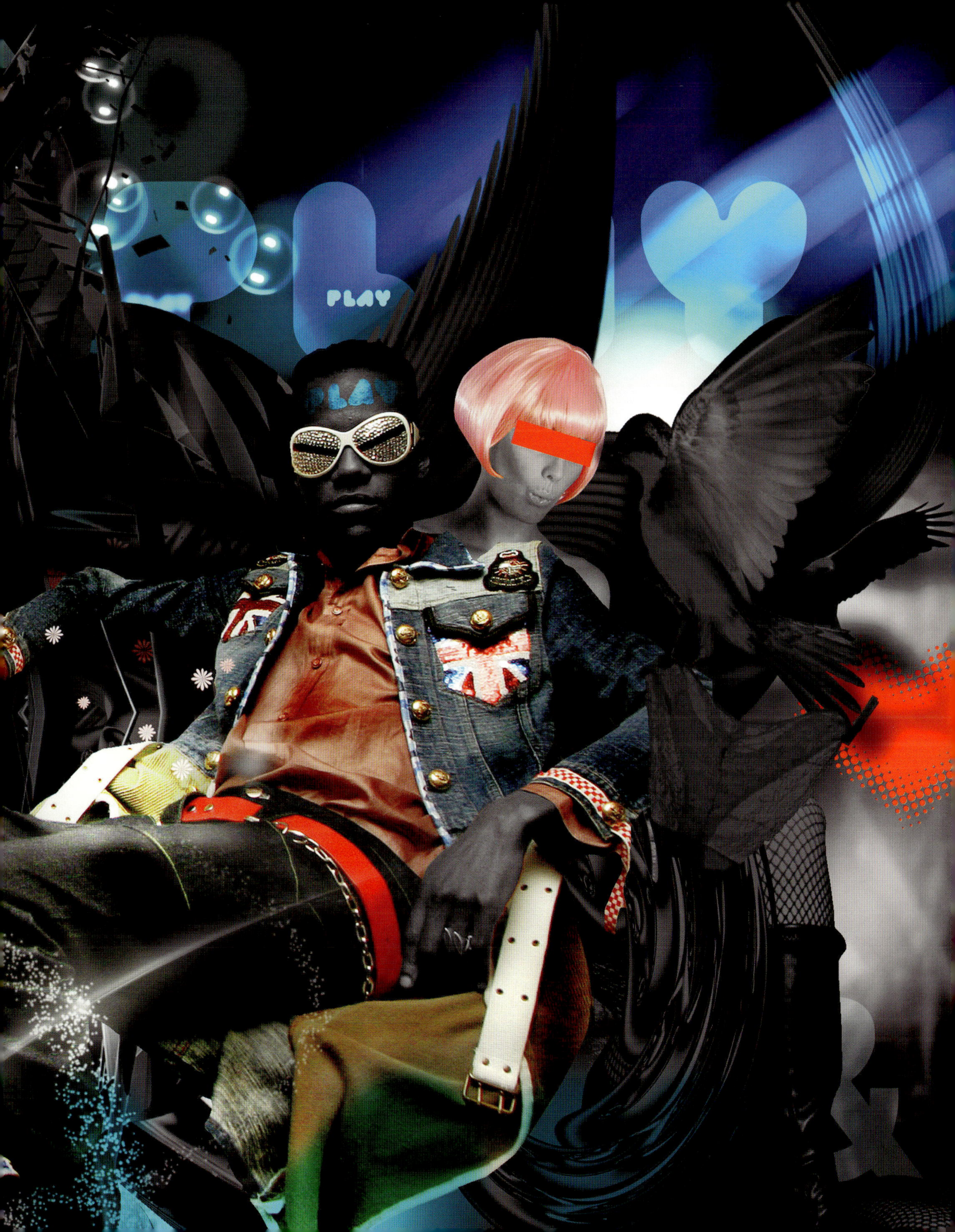
PLAY
PLAY

Hip-hop and advertising are inextricably linked, and, having worked for such brands as British Airways, the BBC, and T-Mobile as well as designing his own line of skateboards, Fraser effortlessly bridges this divide, superimposing visually and rhythmically complex layers of digital imagery with every bit as much virtuosity as any leading hip-hop DJ. *Work & Play*, 2009, combines all of the traditional signifiers of the hip-hop lifestyle into the *sanctum sanctorum* of hip-hop life, the VIP lounge. However, in this work deemed "experimental" by Fraser, the viewer is confronted with a fantasy of what that space could be. The two male figures that make up the central part of the composition are enthroned and surrounded by wings reminiscent of the eagle adorning the throne of Zeus. These are the gods of the hip-hop lifestyle complete with a pink-haired club goddess. The extravagance of hip-hop, the exclusivity of its upper realms, contrasts potently with the neighborhood women portrayed in Sofia Maldonado's 42nd Street mural.

Other artists are even more explicit in their treatment of the bling and commodification of hip-hop culture. The New York-based artist Nadine Robinson is largely known for her large-scale sound sculptures and Boom paintings that reference the boom box of early hip-hop. In her *Study for Bling Bling Boom*, 2004, Robinson constructs "speakers" out of Swarovski crystals, making an overt statement on the commodification of hip-hop. Hank Willis Thomas has gone even farther, equating the commodification of hip-hop with the commodification of the individual through the consumption of brands. In *Branded Head*, 2003, perhaps the best known image from Thomas's larger series *B®ANDED*, the artist presents a stark depiction of a shaved African American man's head on which the Nike swoosh has been digitally branded. Stating that his interest lies in "the branding of 18th and 19th century slaves to mark slave ownership, and in the 21st century how their descendants perpetuate a state of branded consciousness," Thomas questions the entire commodity culture of hip-hop.[22] In *Branded Head*, Hank Willis Thomas presents the corporations' view of the consumer. He is the anonymous body, young and strong with years of potential consumption ahead of him. Is the brand on the side of his head "real"? Is it the visible act of a man who has constructed a part of his identity through his consumption? Or, is this fully the vision of the corporate master, a stealth mark of ownership visible only to those operating the system? This is the liminal space in which the level of complicity of the anonymous everyman must be negotiated. Is his new brand of slavery wholly for the benefit of white economic needs or has he become a slave to his own consumption?

Luis Gispert also engages with the allure of the brand. In his most recent series of digital images, Gispert layers the traditional genre of landscape onto one of the most conspicuous objects of consumption, the customized car. Perhaps second only to apple pie, the automobile is the quintessential signifier of Americanism. In twentieth-century America, car ownership became not only a symbol of material stability, but also a necessity outside of large urban centers where public transportation was marginalized. Even within the cities where public transportation was available, the allure of owning a car—the freedom and ability to rocket down the highway in pursuit of the American Dream—was fixed in the collective American psyche. Hip-hop, as an expression of American youth, naturally took on luxury cars, the Escalade, the BMW, the Mercedes, the Maybach, as the chariots of its royalty and symbolic locus of its aspirations to fame and fortune.

The car has also always been the weekend hobby for countless Americans, and in the hip-hop age it has become the medium for ever-increasing feats of blinged-out excess. In *L.V. Escalade,* 2009, and *Gucci Gloom*, 2010, what at first glance may appear to be a wholly virtual creation is in fact two digital photographs merged. The interior is of an actual car created with loving detail. The upholstery is, as one might expect, not authentic Louis Vuitton. Rather, it is sourced from the same manufacturers who provide the raw materials for the illegal knockoffs so popular with tourists in New York's Chinatown. The underground, black market aspect to this endeavor meant that Gispert had to go to great lengths to find and then win the trust of the car owners. So brand loyal are many of them that they do not stop with simply upholstering their cars with the counterfeit material, they also use it to upholster their furniture and even themselves by making clothing out of it.[23] Though not as physically extreme as the "branding" exhibited in Hank Willis Thomas's work, the extent to which the brand becomes both a signifier of a certain level of (simulated) social status as well as the raw material for a way of life is compelling.

**NADINE ROBINSON**
*Study for Bling Bling Boom*, 2004
Swarkovski rhinestones, aluminum, paint, canvas, and wood
9¼ x 9¼ x 3½ inches
The Jacqueline Bradley and Clarence Otis, Jr. Collection

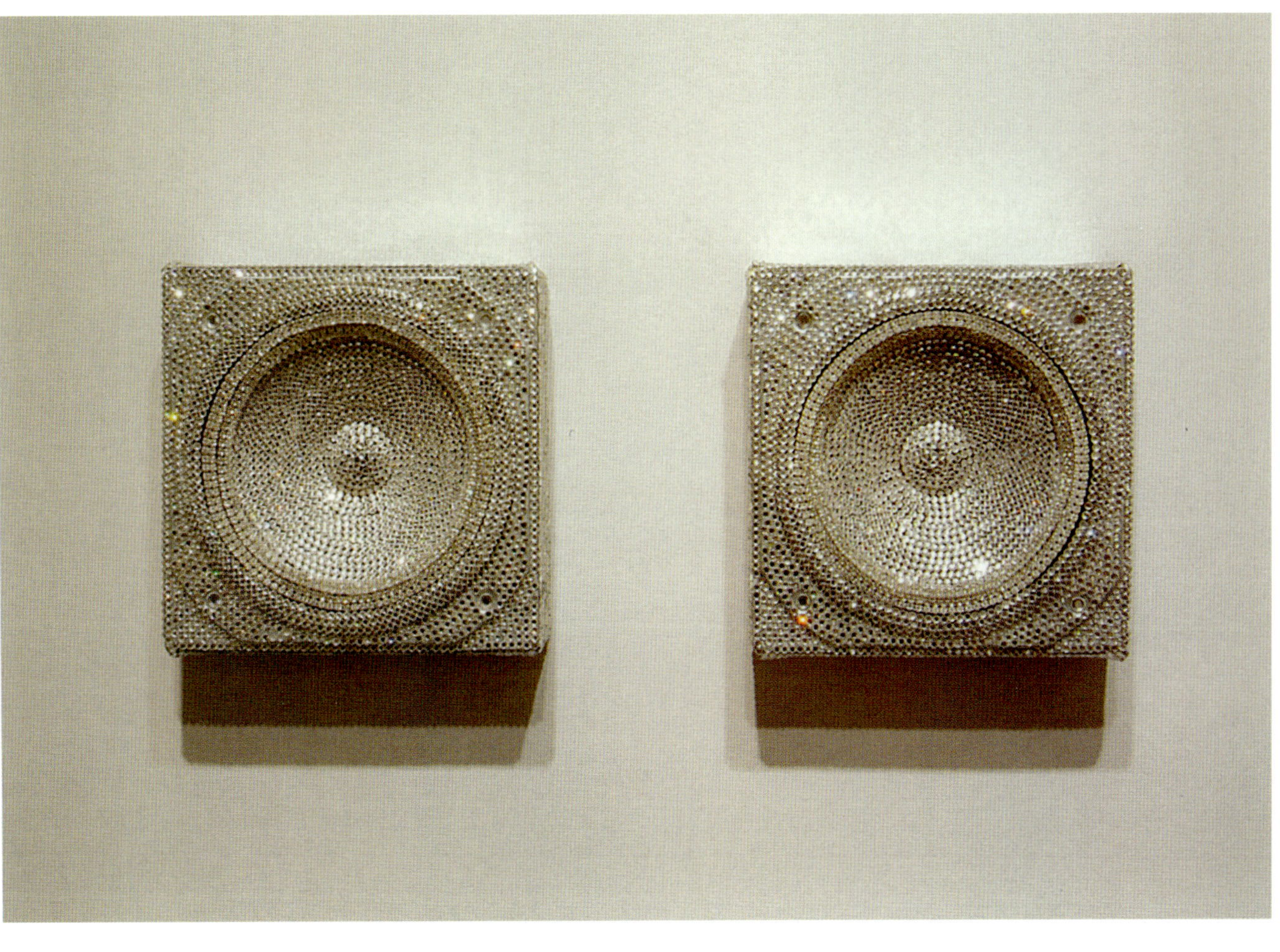

**HANK WILLIS THOMAS**
*Branded Head*, 2003
Lambda photograph
40 x 30 inches
The Jacqueline Bradley and Clarence Otis, Jr. Collection
Courtesy of the artist and Jack Shainman Gallery, New York

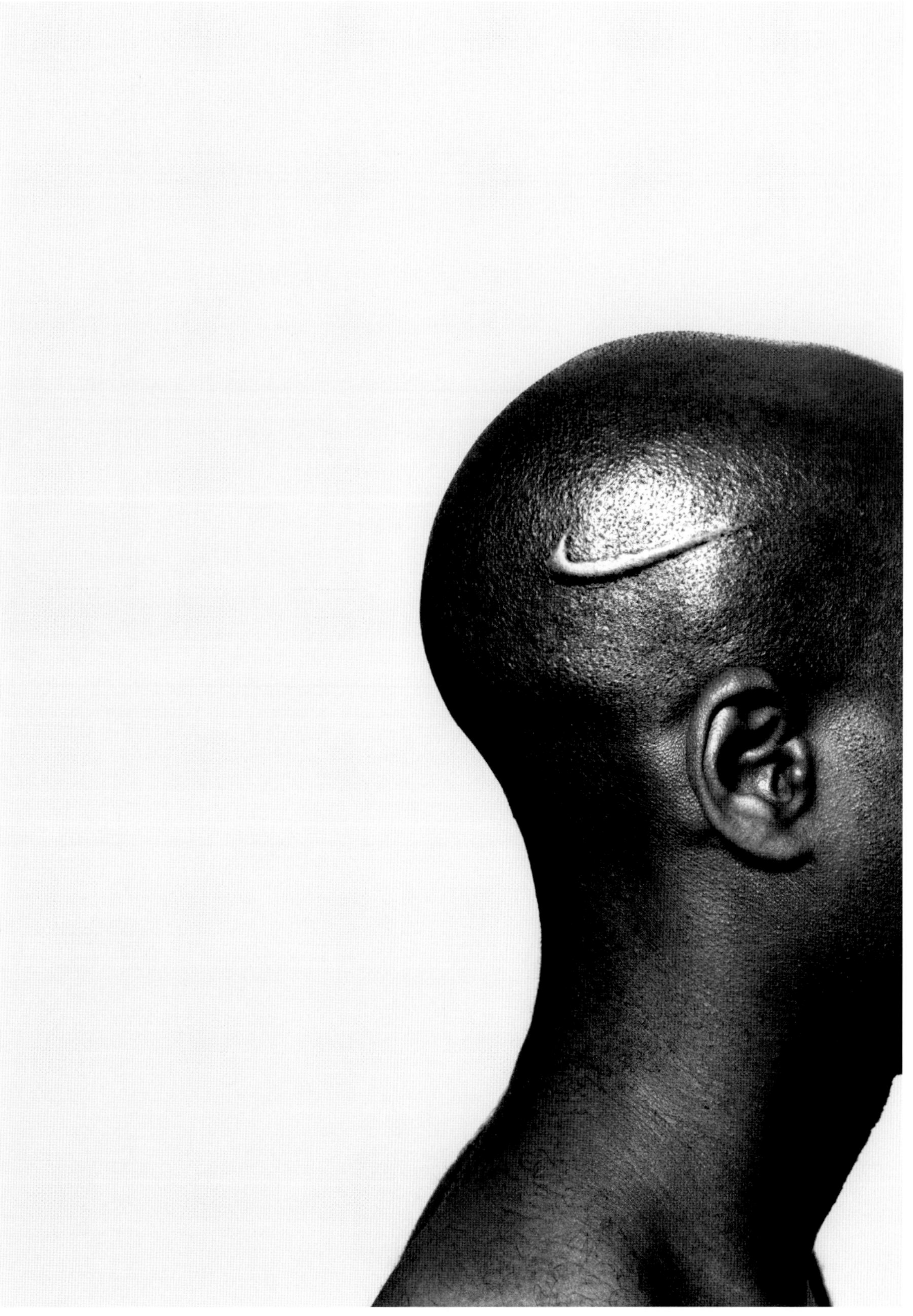

**LUIS GISPERT**
*L.V. Escalade*, 2009
C-print
48 x 72.5 inches
Courtesy of the artist
(detail following pages)

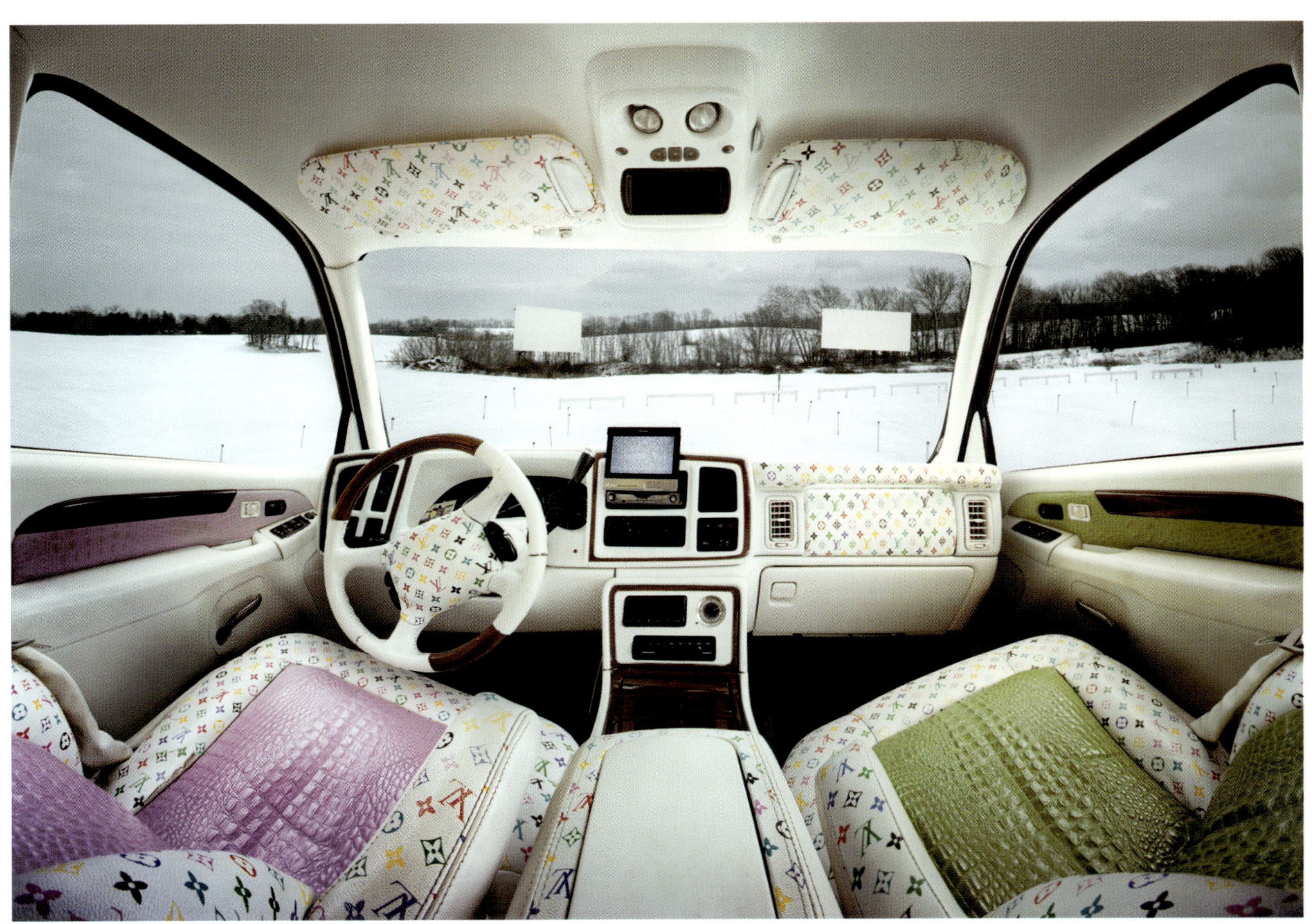

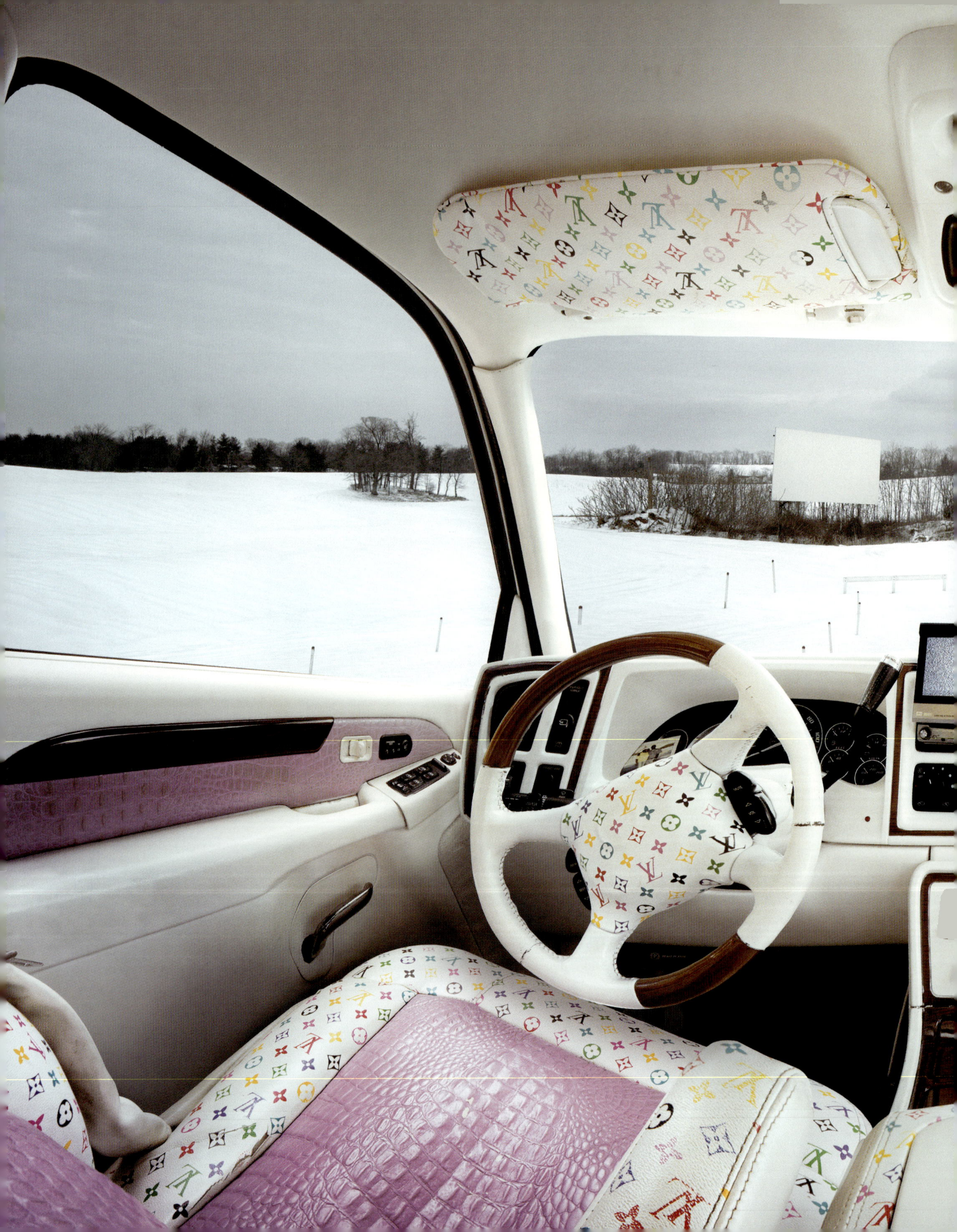

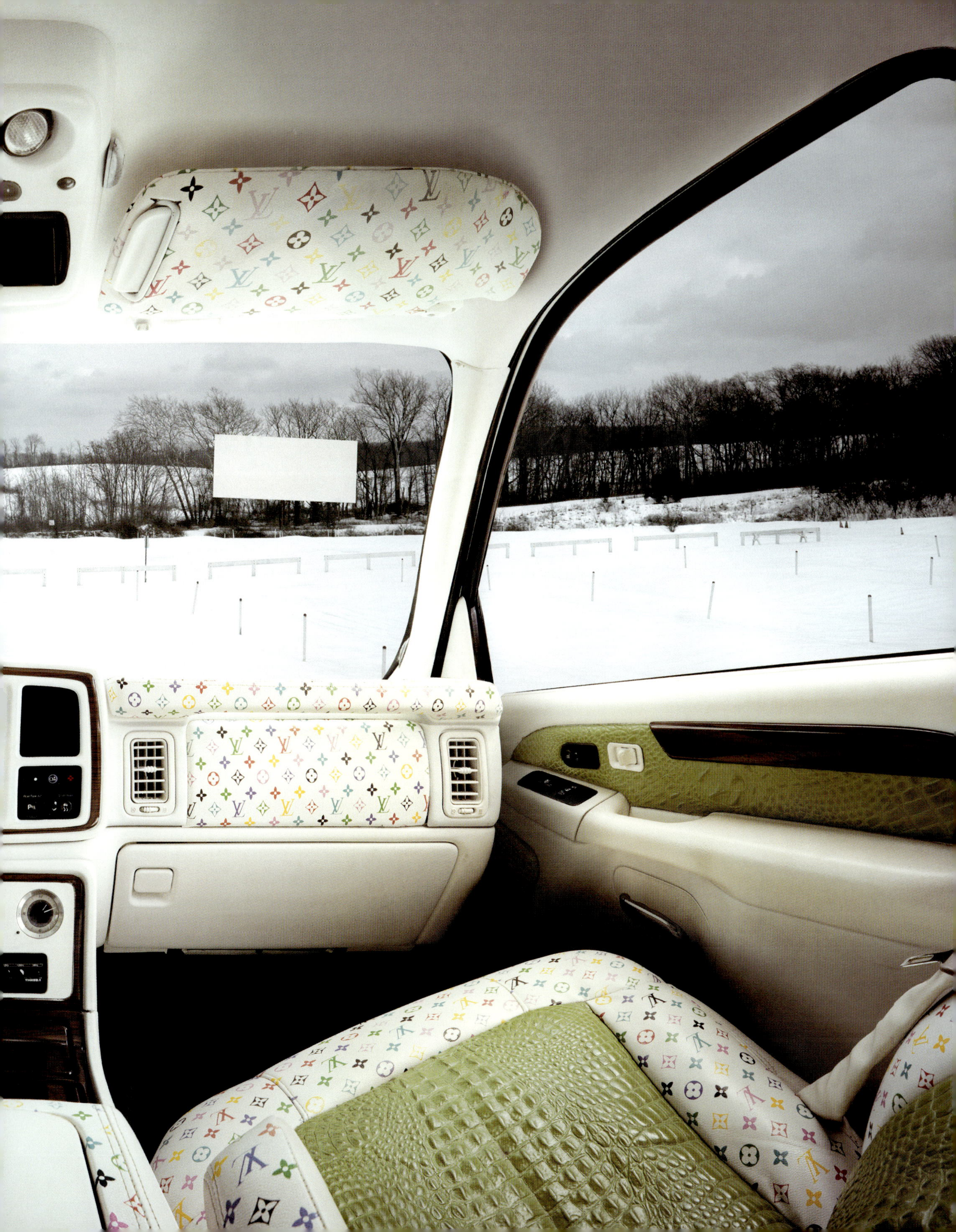

**LUIS GISPERT**
*Gucci Gloom*, 2010
C-print
48 x 63 inches
Courtesy of the artist

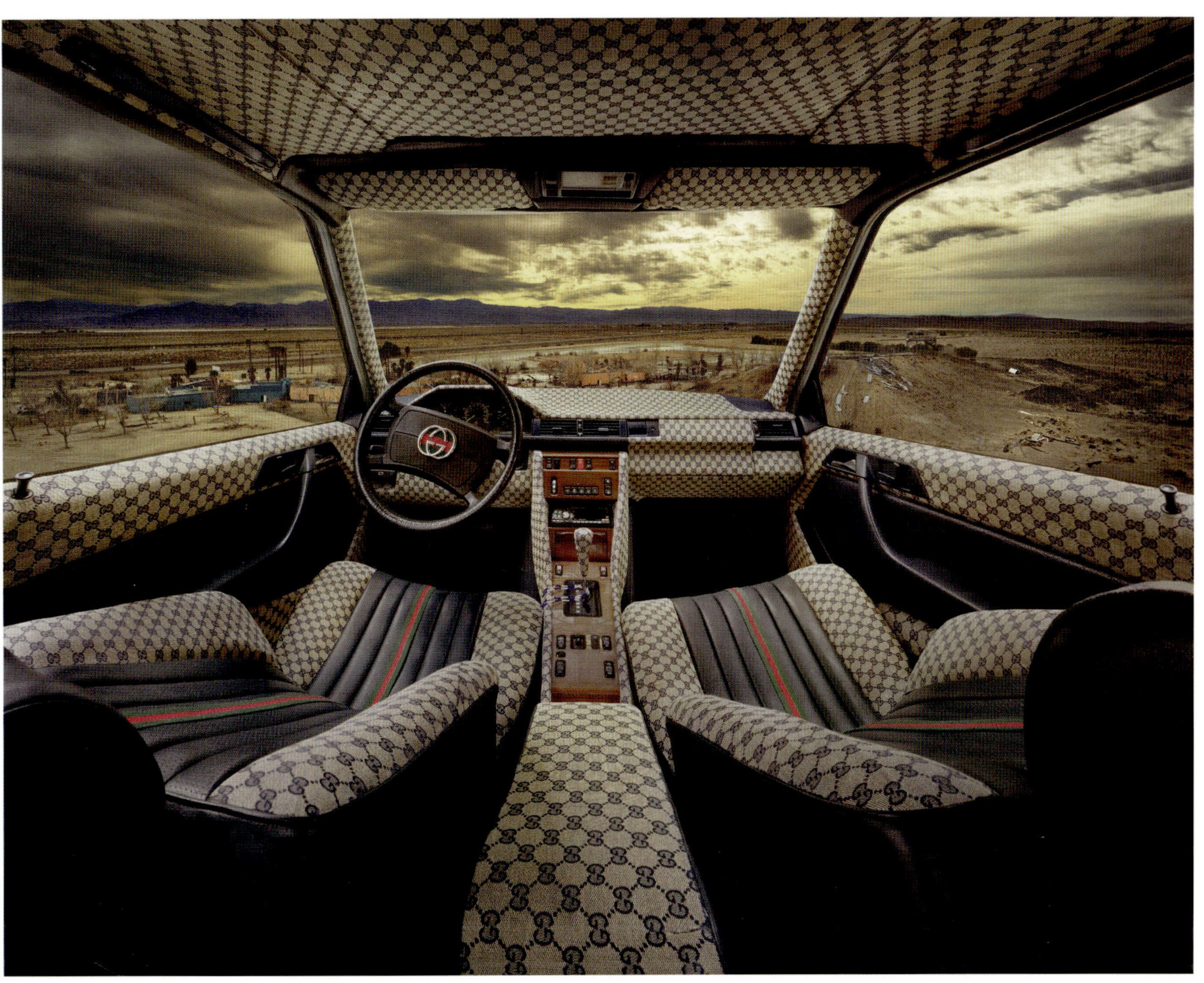

Gispert started this series as a way of experimenting with the canonical genre of landscape within the larger hip-hop context with which his body of work has engaged. In merging the landscape photograph with the interior of the car, he juxtaposes the hard-edged urban aesthetic of bling with the traditional pastoral idyll, the material utopia with the natural utopia. The windows of the car mediate between these public and private spaces but also stand as the historic metaphor of pictorial illusionism reinforcing the illusion of modernism's challenge to the painted surface—the photograph. The digital illusionism of blending two separate photographs into one becomes the ultimate *trompe l'œil*, and Luis Gispert effectively samples from the past as have the other artists discussed here. While conversations with the past are not new to art history, the level of "sampling" and the tremendous diversity of references employed seem a particularly hip-hop aesthetic today.

---

Hip-hop's power, its appeal, is best summed up by one of its founders, DJ Kool Herc. He was there at the very beginning and continues as an elder statesmen of this pan-cultural revolution. "To me, hip-hop says, 'Come as you are.' We are a family... That's why it has universal appeal. It has given young people a way to understand their world, whether they are from the suburbs or the city or wherever."[24] This is what hip-hop tells us, and this is why it will continue to be a powerful influence within the visual arts.

In the thirty-one years since the release of *Rapper's Delight,* hip-hop has become a global force that few, if any, could have ever imagined in the 1970s Bronx streets. Its musical, visual, verbal, and sartorial vocabularies have become a *lingua franca* for nearly three generations, and its economic impact is a consequence with which most of the world's corporations must contend. From its origins in the block parties organized by teenagers, through its translation to a wider, more diverse audience in venues such as the New York night club, The Roxy, and from there to its full-scale global transmission, hip-hop has always been, at its core, an expression of the people. Even when packaged and sold by the Fortune 500, its continued appeal remains its direct, unambiguous street-influenced mode of communication.

The artists discussed here cannot simply be pigeonholed as "hip-hop artists" because there is no single way to define that term. Hip-hop's appeal comes from its diversity and inclusiveness. But, like all of us, they live in a world infused with hip-hop flavors. Whether it is in the street advertising sampled and repurposed by Michael Anderson, or the symbols of consumer desire employed by Hank Willis Thomas, Vince Fraser, and Luis Gispert, hip-hop is all around us and ready to be used in cultural discourses of all varieties. Just as many of our contemporary ideas about women and men are informed by hip-hop, so too are the images of Mickalene Thomas, Kehinde Wiley, and Sofia Maldonado. The hip-hop age of luxury and excess can be viewed in terms of the Western Baroque past in Nadine Robinson's objects of luxury, or in Edo Japan as in the works of Gajin Fujita and iona rozeal brown. The appeal is universal and the influence is all but inescapable. Hip-hop has become the language of the urban block and the suburban lane, the shorthand of the young (and now not-so-young) people of every race and economic background, and, increasingly, it is becoming the language of the gallery inviting each of us to come as we are and engage in direct visual conversations with our presents and our pasts.

## NOTES

1. Nelson George, *Hip-Hop America* (New York: Penguin Books, 1998), 75.
2. Jeff Chang, *Can't Stop Won't Stop: A History of the Hip-Hop Generation* (New York: Picador, 2005), 132.
3. For a thorough discussion of the social contexts of hip-hop's beginnings see: Jeff Chang.
4. Roberta Smith, "Hip-Hop as a Raw Hybrid," *The New York Times*, 22 September 2000.
5. Quote taken from didactic exhibition panel.
6. Lydia Yee and Franklin Sirmans, *One Planet Under a Groove: Hip Hop and Contemporary Art* (Bronx, N.Y.: The Bronx Museum of the Arts, 2001).
7. Roberta Smith, "Out of the Vociferous Planet and in the Orbit of Funk and Hip-Hop," *The New York Times*, 18 January 2002.
8. Greg Tate, "The Golden Age" *The Village Voice*, 16–22 May 2001, 49.
9. Ibid.
10. Derek Conrad Murray, "Hip-Hop vs. High Art: Notes on Race as Spectacle," *Art Journal* 63, no. 2 (Summer, 2004): 7.
11. Excerpted from an interview that appears in this volume.
12. Excerpted from an interview that appears in this volume.
13. This collaborative practice has been linked to traditional Japanese working methods associated with *ukiyo-e* prints of the Edo period. See: Elizabeth Dunbar, "Windswept," in *Zephyr: Paintings by Gajin Fujita*, ed. Elizabeth Dunbar (Kansas City: Kemper Museum of Contemporary Art, 2006).
14. Elizabeth Dunbar also discusses the hybridized kabuki-sports imagery in Fujita's work as a symbolic analogy between *ronin* (masterless samurai) and the graffiti crews and gangs of contemporary L.A.
15. Ibid., 14.
16. Dorothy Shinn, "Artist takes aim at Japan's hip-hop culture," *Akron Beacon Journal*, 28 March 2010.
17. Taken from the artist's statement, "Some words for all of ya'. . ." responding to the controversy. This, as well as numerous internet postings concerning the 42nd Street mural controversy can be found on Maldonado's blog at www.sofiamaldonado.com
18. For a discussion of this within modernism see: Petrine Archer-Straw, *Negrophilia: Avant-Garde Paris and Black Culture in the 1920s* (London: Thames & Hudson, 2000).
19. Excerpted from an interview that appears in this volume.
20. As his profile has been raised, Wiley has produced a number of portraits of celebrities, most notably the VH1 2005 Hip-Hop Honors honorees as well as his monumental portrait of Michael Jackson, commissioned by the pop star but painted posthumously, which was the stand-out statement at Art Basel Miami 2009.
21. "Kehinde Wiley," interview by M.I.A., *Interview*, 2008.
22. Excerpt from artist's statement which can be found on www.hankwillisthomas.com
23. The details were provided in a conversation with the artist 9 July 2010.
24. Jeff Chang, *Can't Stop Won't Stop: A History of the Hip-Hop Generation*, 2005, xi.

# INTERVIEW WITH MICHAEL ANDERSON

**Matthew McLendon:** You did not go to art school, and, I believe, took a life drawing class at college at the suggestion of a girlfriend. What lead you to becoming an artist?

**Michael Anderson:** I think I was always an artist, but I mostly played music when I was younger and never thought about the visual arts. Music was always my first love, and I enjoy playing the drums, piano, and guitar. But, unfortunately, the arts were looked down upon in my house as I was growing up. I was expected to be an athlete and do something professional. I really wasn't able to do anything else, although I tried. The arts just pulled me in, and I've never looked back.

**MM:** You started out as a painter. How did you arrive at your signature technique of collaging elements taken directly from street posters?

**MA:** I originally began painting with oil paint and making collages simultaneously although I didn't know how they would combine from the start. I began by making collage borders out of street posters for my paintings, and, as I progressed, I began to leave spaces open inside of the painted parts and placed the collage into their interstices. I have never collaged on paint or painted on collage, as many artists do. I have a friend, Max Strum, who is a poet, and who told me early on, that eventually I would make only collage and dispel with the painting entirely. I thought he was crazy at the time, but his prediction did come to pass.

Collage is all about collecting, and in the beginning I only used whatever street posters I found immediately. I would rip down a section of posters from the street and put them into water and separate them and use whatever came out directly without any filter. As my collage practice expanded and continued, I began to separate and dry and save different types of imagery and colors and put them into folders for future use. At this point I have been collecting posters for about twenty years and have an incredible collection of saved street posters that allows me the freedom to make almost anything that I can think of. This degree of flexibility is very important to my practice. With painting, you can buy as much blue or red paint as you like, but with collage you have to actually have collected the material you are going to use in order to make any individual collage.

Another big difference in my collage practice is that I use street posters, which are of a much larger scale than the traditional medium of magazines so my collages are much larger than most. Also, one of the main aspects of collage that I think is interesting is that you can play with scale within the composition in ways that would be next to impossible to paint. Scale and perspective are things that, within collage, have been practically eliminated. When painting with pictures, which is how I think of my collage practice, it is possible to have situations and compositions that would be very difficult, if not impossible to achieve in painting.

I am attempting to elevate the respect level of collage to that of the more traditional and storied medium of painting. I feel as though I make paintings, even though my work is made entirely of paper. Many people have told me that they love my paintings, never even realizing that they are collages.

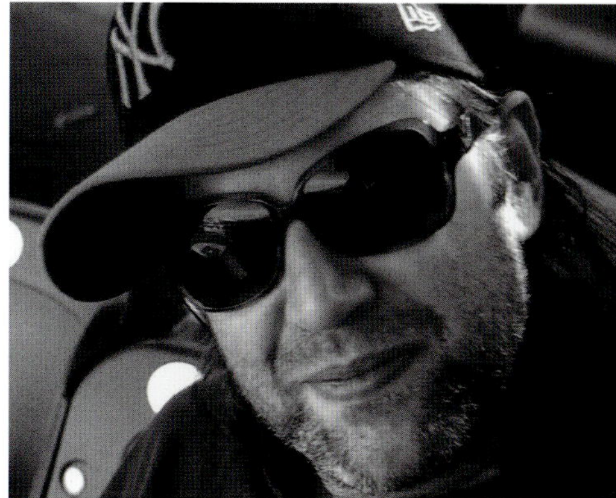

Photo courtesy of Claire Oliver | New York

**MM:** Collage though has a long and respected history within the context of Western modernism. Does this history influence your work?

**MA:** Of course the history of collage has affected me tremendously. I have always been a fan of Romare Bearden, who I consider my old grandpappy in the collage game. His work is amazing, and I've always liked the way he composed his larger pieces, like "The Block" because he got so many stories and situations within an individual composition. This is something that I admire in his work and try to emulate within my own style. I also like many painters for their compositional styles and am influenced by them as well. I am a big fan of Max Beckmann, Francis Bacon, Jackson Pollock, Mark Rothko, Jean-Michel Basquiat, Picasso, and many others. I am supremely interested in abstraction as well as representation and try to use both in my compositions equally, thus the penchant for abstract painters as well. I like Kandinsky a lot, too. His retrospective show at the Guggenheim museum here in NYC last year was very inspiring. I also am a big fan of the affichistes "décollage" movement from

France and Italy in the 1950s and 1960s. Mimmo Rotella and Jacques Villeglé are two of my favorites from that period. I have taken their idea of ripping down posters from the street to make art, but I sort the posters from one another by soaking them in water and recombining hundreds of posters and multiples to really compose pieces directly. I owe them an artistic debt in my gestation as an artist for sure.

**MM:** It's interesting that you cite Kandinsky and Pollock as influences as there is a tension between abstract patterning and the figurative in your work. Are you conscious of this when working?

**MA:** Absolutely. I always employ both abstraction and representation in all of my work because I feel we already have Jackson Pollock and Lucian Freud, who I consider to be the best purely abstract painter and the best purely figurative painter in the history of art, so my intention is to create work that bridges both ideas. I find that many of my favorite contemporary artists are using both together to make new aspects in art.

There are two types of abstraction—abstraction taken from representation or reality, like Kandinsky, or total abstraction (illustrating everything and nothing all at once), like Pollock. I like to try to use both in different ways, depending on the compositional situation. I use abstraction to both fill in the backgrounds of my piece and to tie the imagery together using color and shape. I think a lot about the spaces that will be filled with abstraction because the composition requires that the collage be balanced, so I tend to make the spaces for my abstraction as a direct result of the creation of the representational aspect of a given composition, filling the spaces left in an improvisational manner, which creates a kind of tension and life in the artwork. There is a simple energy that forms when the outcome of the abstraction is unknown at the start of a piece. I am very interested and influenced by jazz and the improvisational styles employed by great musicians. There is something wonderful and surprising about abstraction, in the making of it, this is very exciting to me.

I mostly use the idea of total abstraction but have used representational abstraction as well. For the background abstractions in my work I usually use texts that say something like "in stores now" or "coming soon" or other very banal phrases of modern advertisement. I take these phrases and abstract them entirely, creating what I consider to be "abstract graffiti." In the same way graffiti is made up of letters disguised in unusual ways to create almost a code that can be read only by the initiated, I like to abstract the letters so completely that they cannot even be recognized as letters, but instead become beautiful color passages in my collages.

**MM:** The link with graffiti you've just made is really interesting because in a very concrete way your work is not only influenced by the streets but it is taken from the streets. How do you negotiate the transition from street art to "fine" or "gallery" art?

**MA:** I don't think of myself as a street artist at all, although the street is my palette; I am just using contemporary advertising to create fine art—the materials just happen to be on or from the street. Also, street art is placed on the street, something I never do. I've always felt that the biggest mistake of graffiti has been that the artists always give away all of their work for free. This is the reason why I am not personally a street artist. I am trying to make a living, as difficult and preposterous as that may be as an artist, and I prefer to show my work in galleries and museums because I feel as though the context of my work is strengthened conceptually by exhibiting in a gallery rather than the street. It's always better, I feel, when materials, or ideas are juxtaposed, rather than grouped together in the same form.

**MM:** You could be criticized that by appropriating street posters you are in fact "stealing" the work of others. How do you respond to that?

**MA:** No one has ever accused me of stealing the work of others. The images I take can be thought of in the same way that music samples older music, changing it into a new song, melody, or background, just by changing the context. My friend David La Chappelle has made hundreds of album and magazine covers, and I often use his imagery when it appeals to me. He has told me personally that he thinks what I'm doing is great. I think it falls under the same idea that Warhol employed when he painted a Campbell's soup can—these images are out in the world and are part of our lives. The idea and structure of beauty has shifted and expanded over time, due to relationships between imagery. Context is the root of combining imagery in collage. Picasso also said that the greatest artists are all thieves, so I guess we can look at this idea in different ways.

**MM:** Your titles tend to evoke narratives. How strong is the narrative content of your work?

**MA:** Titles are sometimes the most difficult part of making a collage for me. I create non-linear narratives in my compositions, which can follow a number of story lines in any given collage. I often think of multiple ways of thinking of the relationships between images in pieces, and there is never only one direct way to interpret one of my artworks. The non-linear idea comes from the way that our society actually is. We flip between channels rapidly and search the Web by jumping from one site to another—this is the basis of the modern non-linear narrative. Often I use imagery in a given collage because it fits formally into the composition that I am creating at the time, because composition, to me, is the most important aspect of an artwork. The balance and harmony (or disharmony) that is created in a composition are tantamount to the success of the artwork, in my opinion, so many times the story lines develop as I am putting the elements together to make a collage. Usually when I'm finished with a work I will hang it in the studio and look at it for a month or more and think about all the story lines that I've produced in the piece and try to come up with a snappy title that can be as ambiguous as the piece. I really enjoy when people try to put the stories together and interpret the artwork for themselves. When people ask me if a given collage means this or that, unless they are completely off the mark I always say that they are correct in a certain way, because nine times out of ten, I've thought of their interpretation as one line of reasoning during the creation of the work. I usually imagine five or more ways that the work can be interpreted while I am working on a piece and welcome other interpretations as well. My work is very open.

**MM:** Hip-hop has been criticized for furthering misogynistic views and negative racial stereotypes and some of your work, like *Tropical Fantasy*, could arguably be viewed in this way. How do you feel your art should be interpreted within these contexts?

**MA:** My work is not misogynistic, and people have not criticized it as such. I make such a wide range of collages with differing themes and about different ideas that it has never come up. In all reality though there are many situations in this world that portray women as objects, and if anything, through my work I am illustrating the world we live in now. This I believe is the job of an artist, and I am just the filter that the world is pushed through into my compositions. I also have collages that show women as super-powerful as well. The collage *Tropical Fantasy* can be looked at from two angles, the first being the guys who live on the islands, looking for a beautiful woman who is on vacation in their tropical paradise to have some fun with, but it could also be looked at from the vantage of the rich beautiful women who go to the islands to find a quick fun lover and then leave. Either way the "fantasy" aspect of the collage is in the mind of the individual viewer I suppose.

**MM:** What excites you in contemporary art today?

**MA:** My favorite thing that excites me about contemporary art, and which I think is the most important aspect in a broad way, is the usage of both representation and abstraction simultaneously in picture making. Obviously as well, I am personally excited about the explosion of collage art in this period, too. Collage is a contemporary move in the arts due to the incredible amount of printed material produced by society these days.

## INTERVIEW WITH VINCE FRASER

**Matthew McLendon:** Growing up, what are your first memories of art?

**Vince Fraser:** Since a very early age I always loved drawing. In primary school I illustrated a Marvel-style comic strip and made it into a huge poster in black and white. I remember clearly because it was hung in the corridor and everyone in the school including my teachers was amazed that I actually drew it. Looking back now, I have to admit I was pretty amazed too! Even then I had a keen eye for detail and it definitely shows today in my work.

**MM:** When did you know that you wanted to be an artist?

**VF:** Probably at the age of thirteen when I became interested in design at school. I had a really amazing Art and Design teacher, and then realized I wanted a career as an artist or designer. I have always loved making things and expressing myself in three dimensions so I guess I was pretty lucky.

**MM:** You have worked largely in the commercial world yet your art very easily translates into the gallery. Do you feel stigmatized as a "commercial" artist?

**VF:** No, not really. I've always seen myself as someone who communicates an idea. Originally working as an illustrator, communication was a part of my job. Recently, though, I'm doing more non-commercial commissioned art, which is very different, perhaps with less emphasis on explicit communication.

**MM:** Do you think your work is any different than "fine" art?

**VF:** I think "fine" art is art that is created for the aesthetic principles of art as opposed to "commercial" art that's used for selling, including commercial photography. Graphic art is also considered to be in this category as most graphic artists usually create for websites, stores, and companies rather than primarily expressing themselves through the art. For me, this is a hard question because I'm torn between both. My earlier works were purely for commercial purposes—mainly creating stuff for corporate companies. Now I'm beginning to have more creative freedom and experiment with personal pieces.

**MM:** Is the gallery the right context for what you do?

**VF:** Initially no. But recently I'm becoming more accustomed to the idea of having my work displayed in a gallery. I think this is partly because I now have the freedom to do more experimental works that are more personal and aesthetically pleasing to me. I think this could fall into the category of fine art because they are one-off pieces geared more towards my thoughts and emotions and not a particular commercial market.

**MM:** Are you comfortable there?

**VF:** Maybe in a few years time?

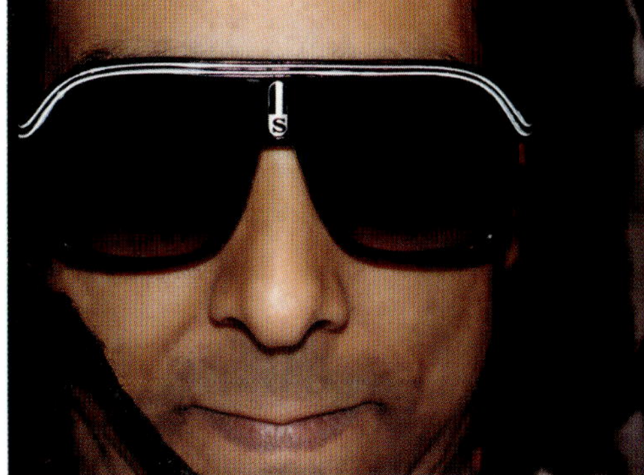

Photo courtesy of the artist

**MM:** I came to know your work from the poster you produced for the 2010 Sarasota Film Festival. As soon as I saw it, I started thinking about you for *Beyond Bling: Voices of Hip-Hop in Art*. You've done work for hip-hop events, but do you think of yourself as an artist influenced by hip-hop culture?

**VF:** I wouldn't say my work is entirely influenced by hip-hop but my work does have references to urban music. I think the whole hip-hop culture is something hard to ignore as it gets such wide media coverage and affects our lives on a daily basis. Listening to music, whether it's hip-hop or house, is an engaging experience for me. It can significantly affect my mood and take over my mind. I would like to think my work delivers a similar engaging experience.

**MM:** In America we tend to think hip-hop began in the Bronx and then, largely due to the Sugar Hill Gang's single *Rapper's Delight* in 1979, that hip-hop spread to the rest of the world. Were you aware of hip-hop "arriving" in the UK?

**VF:** Oh yeah, I remember listening to Eric B and Rakim whilst studying for my diploma in the late eighties. Back then it was still pretty new so it wasn't that popular but still had a small dedicated following in London.

**MM:** Do you think that a type of hip-hop expression may have formed in London simultaneous with New York? After all, hip-hop in the Bronx was influenced by Jamaican and Caribbean immigrants and that culture was even more abundant in the UK at the time.

**VF:** Yes, Jamaican music in particular has been very influential in the evolution of hip-hop. The punk /rock scene was hugely popular in the UK too at the time and saw reggae as a notable influence. Having evolved from ska/rock steady in the late sixties it soon changed into several sub-genres and fusions known as dub and lovers rock, which later developed into hip-hop and rap by people like Jamaican DJ Kool Herc in New York City.

**MM:** Do you think the UK has developed its own, unique hip-hop or does it largely import American styles?

**VF:** The UK definitely has its own style. Grime is huge in the UK at the moment, even my sixteen-year-old son listens to it. It's a fusion of hip-hop, UK garage, and dancehall rhythms, which first emerged in East London in the early 2000s. Combining lyrics with futuristic electronic samples and dark bass lines, it's hugely popular with the younger generation and has even started to make it into the mainstream commercial charts. Some people call it "an amalgamation of UK garage with a bit of drum'n'bass, a splash of punk and a touch of hip-hop thrown in for good measure."

**MM:** As a digital artist you are able to manipulate and appropriate imagery in a way that, at least superficially, is similar to appropriation and manipulation in hip-hop music. Have you ever thought of your work in these terms?

**VF:** Of course, in the same way I fuse two different elements together to create something new and unique, hip-hop icons like RUN DMC did the same revolutionizing a new hybrid sub musical genre called rap / rock with Aerosmith.

**MM:** Do you feel a connectedness between your visual art and music then?

**VF:** Yep, I think music and art go hand in hand. In fact music is a form of art. Music has a significant effect on its listeners, and is used to inform the masses and can even influence the way we dance, dress and even talk. To some degree art has a similar effect because it also influences and affects the senses, emotions and thoughts of the viewer.

**MM:** What do you feel are the primary influences in your work?

**VF:** I find that living life and observing people along the way is a hugely influential factor on my work. My natural determination has taken me to places that have helped me develop as a person and as an artist. I think that situations that take you out of your comfort zone are the ones that teach you and therefore influence you the most. It never ceases to amaze me how many different points of view you discover along the way and how much you can learn when you try to see things from a different perspective.

**MM:** Your images are composed of many layers and are extremely intricate in design. How do you approach a project? What's your working method?

**VF:** I try to research as much as I can into each project so I can create something new and original which is a lot harder than it sounds. I think a lot of artists become complacent over time , cease to be innovative and cease to grow. When that happens, you cease to be an artist. Common pitfalls are people not spending the right amount of time to observe and research a particular subject. My usual working method consists of preparing some hand drawn sketches before embarking on the initial concept stage via my computer. Usually I will have a clear vision of what I'm trying to achieve which makes whole process a lot easier. The other way is to dive straight in and experiment and develop something from scratch, which I try to avoid. Either way, it is the idea that drives the work, and that can come at any point in the project?

**MM:** Hip-hop has been criticized throughout its history for being "too commercial." Do you think, as someone that works in this commercial aspect, that this is a fair criticism.

**VF:** Yes.

**MM:** Do you think that by being commercial hip-hop loses its power of societal critique?

**VF:** It does seem to have changed so much over the years catering to the consumer that it has lost the essence for which it was originally created. To a certain extent I think it has now joined the mainstream that had once excluded its originators. At the same time real hip-hop will always exist too and it's always going be relevant, because there are always real people who care about voicing real issues. Hip–hop is a way of communication, a way of expression and a way of spreading information. It's the voice of the people and what they're going through.

**MM:** What excites you in contemporary art today?

**VF:** There's so much good art out there undiscovered. I tend to like both digital and traditional art. The great part about art for me is that it's a multi-sensory process; I can be drawn to a work because of its technical prowess as well as its simplicity. For me, if it makes me say " wow " then it passes my test! If you look at a piece today and it still looks great ten years later then you know that's great art. Timeless. What makes great art is a strong concept combined with technical excellence. Being self-taught I'm very passionate about improving my skills and bringing it to the next level.

# INTERVIEW WITH GAJIN FUJITA

**Matthew McLendon:** Your father was a painter and your mother restores Asian antiques, so it is fair to say that you grew up in a creative household. When were you aware that you wanted to be an artist?

**Gajin Fujita:** You know, I must have indirectly known when I first started to go out in elementary school and started to mess around tagging outside on the streets because we had to get shipped out, or bussed out, to a different area. That was probably when I had indirect notions of wanting to become a painter or an artist.

**MM:** So it really came directly out of viewing graffiti beginning in elementary school?

**GF:** Yes, I wasn't quite captured or interested with just viewing my father's works or, at that time, my mom wasn't even close to restoring antiques, so it was mostly influence from my dad, having to watch him paint and stuff in our domesticated studio here. But that wasn't really giving my brother and I an interest in fine art. What really did it was the excitement of being mischievous outside on the street and having to feel that rush or that excitement of being stealthy and, you know, trying to pull off this vandalizing type of thing—that really caught my attention.

We live in a Latino gang culture here in Boyle Heights, and they've been around for a long time so their tags or their monikers or gang name and territory rights, and all of this, have been being painted for a long, long, time in this area. [During] that period I probably thought it to be more of a negative, you know, vandalizing people's property probably through the parental influence always saying, "why are they always painting the side of our house?" It wasn't until I must have been like thirteen or fourteen and started to realize that there were aesthetics to all of this, styles, and how different people have different styles and, yeah, that's when it really captivated me.

**MM:** When did you join your first crew?

**GF:** That must have been about [age] fifteen; it was called the Kids Gone Bad [KGB].

**MM:** And then you went over to Kill to Succeed [KIIS], right?

**GF:** Right. Back when I was fifteen, Los Angeles graffiti had become a phenomenon but only to those who were really excited about hip-hop. It kind of emerged from break dancing and rap music, and it transitioned into doing graffiti afterwards. I think break dancing and the music came a lot earlier than graffiti in L.A. It wasn't until [around] '83 really, when we saw that movie *Style Wars* from New York where it really got kids attracted to graffiti, and kids here were really intrigued by that movie, I think. But then, the movement was still really small, and people knew each other back then, even if you were from rival crews. It wasn't like gangs, so, it was like a friendly rivalry, and we mostly competed amongst each other doing murals, etc. Nothing violent—we all knew each other, and when I was in KGB I was already familiar with KIIS because they were mostly kids from East L.A, downtown. KGB was more from the Hollywood, West Hollywood area, and, yeah, it's funny because even graffiti crews start to break up into regional sections and kind of get a segregation thing going, just like the gangs. I think it comes with the territory here in L.A.; it's just so vast and there's so much territory to cover.

**MM:** You mentioned being raised in Boyle Heights, which is a predominately Latin neighborhood, and you're Japanese American, so did this make you hyper aware of being different from the other kids as one of the few Asian families?

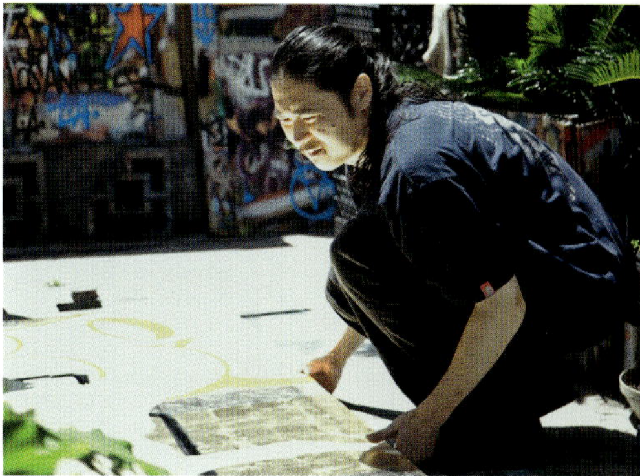

Photo by Jeff McLane

**GF:** Yeah. I mean, I wasn't aware as much as they [were] making me aware.

**MM:** The other kids making you aware?

**GF:** Oh yeah, they were quick. It was probably 98% Latino, and I was the minority amongst the minority. We got the hazing; my brothers and I were just picked on and there was maybe one other family that was Japanese American. There were some Japanese Americans and Jewish Americans that had come in the early '30s and then post-War but in the eighties it was more elderly people, and today there's like absolutely none left [in the area]. It's a pretty interesting demographic.

**MM:** Do you think being the "minority among the minority" pushed you toward incorporating Japanese idioms into your work?

**GF:** It probably did. I wasn't acutely aware or intending for it to be that way, I don't think, but it probably had like a natural influence, me wanting to kind of fuse the two cultures, like the Latin American culture that I grew up in and the Japanese culture that I was influenced by at home.

**MM:** How do you identify yourself? Do you think of yourself as American, or Japanese American, or Japanese? Do you consciously even think about that?

**GF:** I don't even try to think about it, and it doesn't really come up into my conscious, but I do think I'm an American with a mixture of all these cultures as well as L.A. being a bridge to the Pacific—I think it's the epitome of being American.

**MM:** Everyone obviously talks about the Japanese influence in your work as well as graffiti; do you think that there are other influences that have not been recognized or talked about sufficiently?

**GF:** You know, you're right. A lot of people do talk about the Japanese culture being fused with the graffiti, but I do feel sometimes that graffiti gets this negative connotation, and it's then stereotyped as being vandalistic and somewhat sadistic as well. I can't control other graffiti artists from doing what they want and painting wherever they want, but sometimes I feel like these people shouldn't speak up unless they research this subculture a little bit more. But to each their own. I'm pretty sure they have their own sets of experiences with it whether positive or negative. I'm not trying to please everybody anyway.

**MM:** Do you consider yourself a graffiti artist or an artist who incorporates graffiti into his work?

**GF:** When I was younger, I probably considered myself a graffiti artist, but today I consider myself a fine artist, definitely.

**MM:** When you were fourteen you made a trip to Japan with your parents, and you came across *katakana kanji* and *hiragana*, the Japanese writing styles. How did this then affect your graffiti style?

**GF:** The *katakana* and the *hiragana* were embedded in our childhood with my parents trying to teach us Japanese, first and foremost, so English was almost like a second language when we went to preschool and elementary school. It wasn't until I was fourteen and had taken trips to Japan that I found out this has a huge aesthetic; this has a style in calligraphy.

**MM:** You talk about seeing the Golden Pavilion in Kyoto, and you have said you thought about what a "violation" it would be if someone tagged it. Also, you studied with Dave Hickey at University of Nevada, Las Vegas, and he told you to "violate" people's expectations with your art. I was struck by the power of this term in relation to graffiti. Do you see your work as "violating" in a way?

**GF:** I try to capture something that can be violating, I think.

**MM:** How do you mean violating, then?

**GF:** I've thought of it as kind of like a shock value; it's like when people are shocked or when I see something that I haven't ever seen before, the first time for people to perceive something in a certain a way—to me I thought that meant violation from what Dave had said to us when I was in school.

**MM:** Something that might be closely related to violation is violence of which there's quite a bit in your work. What role does violence play for you?

**GF:** I think it largely stems from me being raised near Hollywood, or even in the States. In the eighties we were bombarded with action and thriller type movies, and I think that has had a huge influence on me indirectly. It isn't anything I had experienced, hands on, but also living amongst such gang-filled areas, and you hear on the local news such and such gang killed three people last night. The eighties were the height of gang violence, and those kinds of things are the influences of violence in my pictures.

**MM:** I want to get into your process a bit. There is a lot of collaboration in your work. You have your friends come and tag panels, and this is then referred to in scholarship on your work as being linked to the collaborative process of making *ukiyo-e* prints in the Edo period. However, there's also a long tradition of workshops in the Western tradition. Are you conscious of this collaboration in line with these traditions or is it just natural for you coming out of graffiti crews?

**GF:** I think it's the latter. This is really the first time someone has put that in my brain. However, I think it's a great point. But, honestly for me this is coming from graffiti society. It's keeping a genuine experience as well as the process, which stems from the street or painting out in the yards. That's where I came up with the idea of having friends come over and bombard the backgrounds of my paintings.

**MM:** Text obviously plays an important role and can be linked to your ties with graffiti. How do you approach word and image in your art?

**GF:** That is a process that I always toy with, and to this day I've gone through many different phases. When I started producing this type of work back in Vegas when I was a student under Dave [Hickey], I think I was a lot more literal. Today I am having to do away with the text that comes out in the foreground to make it more enigmatic for the viewer to decipher. I don't want to be so literal now.

**MM:** Graffiti, in a way, acts as a code especially to a gallery audience who might be unfamiliar with the tags. I would think that already brings a level of enigma to your work.

**GF:** Right. I also go over a lot of the tags and throw ups that have been painted by my friends or by myself for compositional reasons, but there are definitely hidden texts, or meanings; that's a good point.

**MM:** There have recently been several big museum shows based on graffiti. Do you think graffiti loses its transgressive nature when translated into the museum or gallery?

**GF:** No, I think the transgressive origin is here to stay. Kids out on the streets are always taking it to different heights. I would call them extreme athletes. I think the generation that came after me (they already include me in the old school), are taking it to different heights maybe due to the authorities cracking down a bit harder and the graf artists trying to be more elusive.

**MM:** The graffiti in your work calls attention to another key characteristic of your paintings—surface. You employ gold, silver, and platinum leaf to the panels. In the literature this has been likened to the metallic surface of the subway trains we associate with the early days of graffiti as well as the Golden Pavilion in Kyoto. How do you think about surface when beginning a work?

**GF:** Those ideas have all come across my mind when I start building my surfaces. Surface is especially important to me because of presentation—the finish has to be close to, if not, pristine. Having studied the Finish Fetish artists, when I saw a John McCracken I was in awe to see something so pristine made by hand. I try to quality control my own work in that fashion.

**MM:** Certainly the Finish Fetish aesthetic is something we particularly associate with California.

**GF:** Right, and also it comes from growing up in this car culture that has thrived in California. Also I've done tons of skateboarding and surfing, and it stems from those cultures as well.

**MM:** Your work is also discussed as having an affinity with hip-hop culture. Do you agree with this?

**GF:** Sure, I think my work can be called hip-hop because when I make an analogy of the process of my paintings it's always great to take the people who DJ. Music, I think, is a great parallel. The DJs and musicians of the hip-hop world who created some of the great beats and great songs ingrained in my head from the eighties and nineties, these guys had basically stolen from the classic music. I feel my process is similar to that, but is being done visually.

**MM:** Hip-hop also incorporates a lot of overtly sexual imagery and there is a lot of overt sexuality in your recent work based again on traditional Japanese imagery. What led you to this explicit sexual imagery?

**GF:** That goes back to Dave's [Hickey] violation. I was toying with that notion in my studio in Vegas and it was like an epiphany when I came across the *shunga* prints.

**MM:** Do you see it as tied to modern expressions of gender and sexuality?

**GF:** Yes, sure, I do because these *shunga* prints were actually like the magazines we see today, but I think they were more stealthy about bringing them out in public because the shoguns were trying to do away with that imagery.

**MM:** Can you link this, then, back to hip-hop culture which can be very sexualized and the portrayal of women?

**GF:** I've always thought some of the songs were way out and that's coming from someone that does these types of paintings. I don't think I'm intentionally trying to dog women like that. That's why I think some of the lyrics are too violating.

**MM:** What excites you in contemporary art today?

**GF:** That's a very deep question. From time to time I ask myself, why is somebody like Damien Hirst, or why is somebody like Jeff Koons, or [Takashi] Murakami getting so much attention? Their works are almost not even touched by them. They don't come from a conventional background, though they do follow Andy Warhol's blueprint for making art, but I wonder if one day the person who is making art in the conventional fashion might come out in the foreground? I also like people like Banksy. I think he comes from a real place. I haven't seen his movie, but friends who have seen it tell me he's not really a bad guy, not the typical asshole graffiti artist that people might portray him as. When I heard how grounded and modest he is about himself, I really thought highly of him and what he has been able to accomplish globally. Not to take away from the Jeff Koons and Damien Hirsts of the world, though.

**MM:** For me it's very interesting to hear that someone like you who is so process driven and hands-on is thinking about artists like Koons and Hirst, who are so conceptual and may rarely touch the final product.

GF: Well, maybe I have a slight notion of wanting to become like them one day [laughs] because of what you've just mentioned about my process being so conventional and hands-on. I wish I could have a hundred helpers to assist me—some days I feel like I wish I didn't have to touch that spray can [laughs].

# INTERVIEW WITH LUIS GISPERT

**Matthew McLendon:** When and how did you come to the decision to be an artist?

**Luis Gispert:** I spent the first ten years of my life cooped up in a New York apartment. There was a lot of playing alone time, so I created a world that was always more than the real. Once I left home, "art" seemed like the only viable way to continue to create and live in that world without being arrested or interned.

**MM:** Of all the artists in the exhibition *Beyond Bling: Voices of Hip-Hop in Art* your work is arguably the most overtly influenced by hip-hop. What draws you to hip-hop, and why do you think it has had such a pronounced influence on your art?

**LG:** Being first generation from an immigrant family [from Cuba], popular culture was my access to American culture. A point of departure for many of my projects is to reference things that had great impact on me before I was initiated to understand "art." In the end, my work is like a funnel absorbing everything in the world that interests me. Hip-hop happens to be one of them.

**MM:** Hip-hop has its critics who feel it furthers negative racial stereotypes and objectifies women, among other things. Your work—I'm thinking in particular of the *Cheerleader* imagery from the early 2000s—has engaged with these topics. Do you think the criticisms of hip-hop are fair?

**LG:** That criticism was prevalent in the early 2000s when hyperbole in hip-hop reached critical mass. My work at the time was responding to that phenomenon. I was never interested in making a didactic critique. I opted for a more nebulous stance that hovered between criticism and celebration.

**MM:** You were born in New Jersey, raised in New York and Miami, and now live in Brooklyn. Do you see differing expressions of hip-hop in each of these places?

**LG:** Living in New York until the age of ten saw me close to the birthplace of hip-hop around the late 1970s early 1980s. When I moved to Miami I discovered a new strain of hip-hop, "Booty Bass," a proto-southern hip-hop "crunk." Miami was the first southern American city to define a hip-hop sound different from New York. It was characterized by bass heavy beats and pornographic lyrics.

**MM:** Your work definitely has an "American" feel to it and references fairly specific cultural phenomena. As you travel around the world quite a bit, what reception does your work receive outside of America?

**LG:** Even though my reference points tend to be America specific, I always attempt to make work that transcends my cultural references and touches upon universal themes or moods. In recent years my work has found audiences in England, Germany, Sweden, and Spain. As Americans we underestimate how exotic our culture can be to the rest of the world.

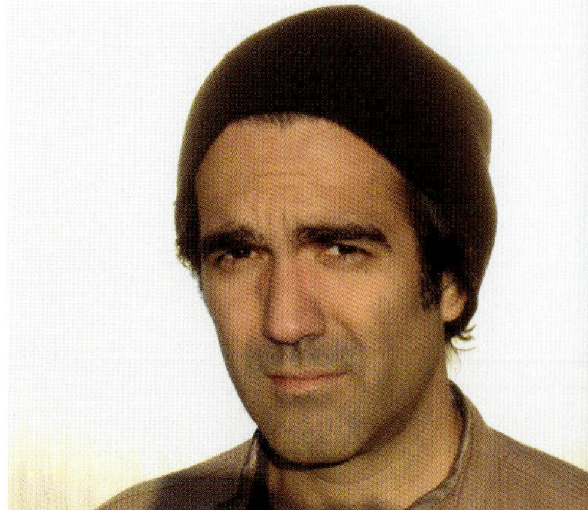

Photo by Diana Al-Hadid

**MM:** You work in a number of different media, sculpture, photography, film—do you have a medium that you feel most comfortable with? Is the diversity of media related to hip-hop's sampling, or is that too superficial a reading?

**LG:** No, consciously it has nothing to do with hip-hop sampling. My practice tends to be schizophrenic as I jump from media to media fitting my moods. I bore easily, my attention span is short, I cycle through hundreds of ideas a week, few see the light of day. I just want to entertain myself, challenge my comfort level. When a project or a series becomes easy, it becomes "work." Showing up to the studio like a factory worker producing widgets is not fun. When that happens I close that body of work and start over.

**MM:** Working across so many media, what particular artists have influenced you?

**LG:** People that come to mind are Andrea Zittel, Bruce Nauman, Max Ernst, Luis Buñuel, Felix Gonzales Torres, The RZA, and Kathryn Bigelow.

**MM:** That's a fairly diverse list. What is it about these artists that interests you?

**LG:** All of these artists questioned and pushed their form.

**MM:** Your latest series explores the customized car subculture. What drew you to this subject?

**LG:** My interest in customized car culture is a biographical one as I participated in it during my adolescence in Miami. My photographic work from 2000 to around 2008 involved the representation of figures or bodies in narrative tableaux. A significant number of those figures were people of color. At some point I began to see it problematic how the representation of these dark bodies were being fetishized and consumed by predominately white art audiences. The work became facile and began to lose the critical gravitas I originally intended for those images. Up to that point my photographic tableaux were fictional and manipulated. I longed for a project that contained some factual documentation of the world. I turned to the exhausted genre of landscape photography as a challenge. The series requires me to seek out customized cars that have very personal connections to their owners. I then travel in search of dramatic sunsets in sublime landscape. Finally, with minimal manipulation, I combine the images to create a proscenium arch for nature with these handmade vehicles interiors.

**MM:** You have confronted the commodification and "bling" inherent in hip-hop in a number of your works such as *No Half Stepping*, 2010. Hip-hop now drives a large segment of consumer culture. Do you think the commodification of hip-hop has lessened its ability to critique society?

**LG:** The commodification of hip-hop has sprouted the question "is hip hop dead?" The relevant question is, "where is hip-hop's vanguard, or underground?" Hip-hop is a popular culture movement by people of color that has found its way into academia and the arts. What's interesting is to see what art is being produced in this new canon.

**MM:** How do you negotiate the relationship between your work's status as "fine" art and the popular, consumerist aspects of hip-hop?

**LG:** There's no conscious negotiation of that relationship. If I did that I would never get anything done in the studio. I work intuitively, all my production is under the guises of art, and how it exists in the world after it leaves my studio is beyond my control.

**MM:** Kehinde Wiley (2001), Mickalene Thomas (2002), iona rozeal brown (2002), and yourself (2001) were all in the MFA program at Yale and you have each emerged with distinct voices yet are all somewhat indebted to hip-hop culture. Did your time at Yale foster this influence this or do you think it was already imbedded in you as products of your generation?

**MM:** I think it's no coincidence that we all ended up in art school in the early 2000s. We are part of the first generation of children who grew up on hip-hop that decided to become visual artists.

**MM:** What did the Yale experience provide you as an artist?

**LG:** Yale's biggest contribution to me was the demystification of the artistic process.

**MM:** What excites you in contemporary art today?

**LG:** I like art that is a question. I'm very excited about the new generation of artists that make no hierarchal distinctions between "low culture" and "high culture." My generation still has an anxiety, or self-consciousness about this hierarchy that was passed on by elitist mentors. I'm looking forward to being perplexed by new metaphors they [the new generation of artists] will create.

# INTERVIEW WITH SOFIA MALDONADO

**Matthew McLendon:** What are your earliest memories about art? When did you know you were an artist?

**Sofia Maldonado:** I've been drawing, painting, working with ceramics, and developing a sense of fashion since I was very young. While I was in high school, living in Old San Juan and surrounded by abandoned colonial buildings, I focused on walls that had an interesting texture, recognizing each building as my canvas.

I would say since I was sixteen I have been working for my future career, always thinking of how to grow as an artist. I remember taking a lunch break and just staying at the studio working while most of the kids were playing on the patio or flirting with the boys.

I would paint with my graffiti writer friends every weekend after school. By the second year of university, I started getting local attention in my country. I got lots of painting gigs in clubs, museums, galleries, etc. Media started approaching me for interviews on TV, radio, and in local newspapers. After I finished my BFA in La Escuela de Artes Plásticas, I decided to head to New York City to do an MFA and continue my career as an artist. That was a great experience cuz' it was like a new beginning. I knew I had to get up again so I focused on developing a consistent studio work practice.

**MM:** Your art incorporates influences of graffiti, hip-hop, skateboarding—all quite urban. Why do these things resonate with you?

**SM:** Those were my surroundings in Puerto Rico; lots of graf/skater friends and I enjoyed making art related to my lifestyle. Also, I developed a thirst for painting over surfaces that people could walk over, and skateboarding was a perfect community to interact with my artwork.

For example *The Tropical Storm Bowl* project consisted of an abandoned pool in the middle of the rainforest that we rescued and painted—then we went there to skate. All this process was filmed.

Moving to New York was a big change for my life and art. Living surrounded by Afro-Caribbean-Latino communities became my new reality, and the work got a twist. Unlike other neighbors, I always try to maintain a friendly environment with the locals. Sometimes I improvise skateboarding art workshops for the kids in my street or open a cinema for the community.

**MM:** What specific influences of hip-hop do you feel are most important to your art?

**SM:** Female fashion and dance moves. I love how we Latinas and black women dance so provocatively/sexy, and we are conscious that it is just a body expression, conserving our femininity. To my surprise, at most of the white kids' parties people only dance when they are wasted.

I praise the body movement and flow of energy in the woman's body when she is in action on the dance floor, on the sidewalk, in a music video, or just walking. It is a beautiful thing that we have in the Caribbean, and in a way I also like to create an reinterpretation of the female character through hip-hop and *reggaeton* culture and how it influences this new generation of girls.

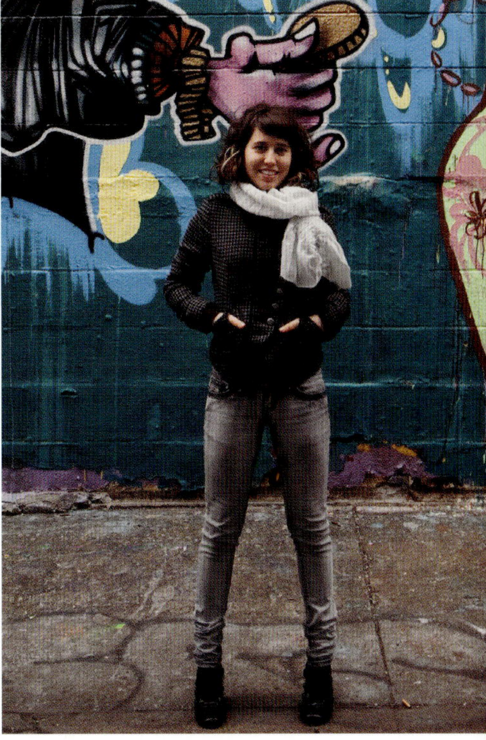

Photograph by Zach Callahan, courtesy of Magnan Metz Gallery, New York

**MM:** Recently, your mural commissioned by the Times Square Alliance for 42nd Street in New York received a great deal of criticism by people who felt the depictions of African-American and Latina women furthered negative stereotypes. You responded that these were the women you know and see regularly, and they should not be judged negatively because of personal style choices. Were you surprised by the criticism the mural received?

**SM:** Yes! Maybe because I come directly from Puerto Rico, we have a different way of appreciating this style of women in our day-to-day [experience]. In the U.S. minority women have been repressed by white people for many years and have been fighting to get accepted in that society. It is totally understandable that they can read my work from the wrong perspective just as the media has portrayed them for years. But I come from a different background, and there is a language, a beauty that I want to represent, which it is not always seen as. The body in the Caribbean is very normal, just like in the dancing: you show it, you move your hips, and rub with your man. It is all part of our culture, and the younger generations have taken it to another level of sensuality. If you live in the Caribbean the [42nd Street] mural would not be such a rare thing or so called "inappropriate visual language."

But there were a lot of people who did understand and admire the work's quality. The mural opened a door of discussion for a few months in New York black/Latino forums. So I think it was a great opportunity and experience!

**MM:** Figures from the mural are now taken out of the original context and placed within the museum/gallery. Do you think this changes their reception at all?

**SM:** This is great, because it will bring the discussion into a new forum. It is an artwork that made history and should be given an importance in history.

**MM:** Mural art has a long history within Latino and Caribbean cultures. What drew you to creating murals?

**SM:** Sometimes I attach to them political messages but very subtle, like the redhead chica in the 42nd Street mural with the knuckle-brace that said "Libertad." A very patriotic act from a Puerto Rican artist in New York! In Puerto Rico, this form of expression is related to students' struggle and the freedom fighters against the colonial government.

**MM:** How do you think the mural functions in contemporary society?

**SM:** Today we have street art. Most of these artists just express their artistic vision. Sometimes they can attach political ideas to their mural expressions, but it is more divided. There are some community organizations that try to educate but they do not carry a militant or revolutionary idea as the Mexican Muralist movement did. Murals have become like free canvases to lots of artists that want to express their vision, and it is beautiful expression. Usually it gets painted over and does not get the respect it should. People need to be more conscious of this expression!

**MM:** Hip-hop culture has been criticized for the objectification and sexualization of women, and the women you depict in your art certainly show an influence of hip-hop in their fashions. Do you feel this criticism of hip-hop is fair and accurate?

**SM:** Yes, hip-hop and *reggaeton* is very *macho* oriented. The females are treated as objects. Most of my references come from this culture, but I have mixed feelings on how this affects society. If you live in that scene that is pretty much your "reality," and that is where my artwork comes into play. Funny thing is that media advertisements do the same and *do not* get criticized as much, especially if non-voluptuous females are involved.

**MM:** How do you, as a Puerto Rican woman, negotiate what have historically been male-dominated arenas such as hip-hop, skateboarding, and graffiti?

**SM:** I am half Cuban and Puerto Rican and that makes me a really strong-workaholic-woman. If you are focused on your work, not the lifestyle, when you are in these male-dominated arenas there are more chances to get respected.

**MM:** Do you view yourself as an artist or as a woman artist?

**SM:** ARTIST . . . always have, but deep inside you know it is double the work.

**MM:** Your most recent series, *Concrete Jungle Divas*, is comprised of five portraits of what might best be described as hip-hop divas. Why did you choose these five in particular?

**SM:** Because they were the five that were blasting the radio or the local news for some personal drama at a particular time. And I also picked them because of their cultural background: Beyoncé—American; J-Lo [Jennifer Lopez]—Puerto Rican; Rihanna—Caribbean; M.I.A.—activist ideals; and Lady Gaga—the white bitch . . . And they all have some sort of connection to hip-hop, fashion, female diva (and the woman that I generally paint is inspired or tries to be her look-a-like). This time I went to the target that inspires or rules fashion on the streets of my neighborhood.

**MM:** Growing up in Puerto Rico and now living in New York, what do you perceive as differences in hip-hop culture and expression between the two places?

**SM:** If your are not in a Latino neighborhood you will not listen to any auto-tune *reggaeton* hits . . . I used to miss that so much while living in BedStuy [Bedford-Stuyvesant]. But that neighborhood inspired me in lots of ways, and I learned about them and how different it is from the Afro-Caribbean culture I came from.

**MM:** Has living in New York influenced your work?

**SM:** Yes! It mostly changed the style of my female characters and developed much love for BedStuy and its street characters. I ended up dressing more Latina with doorknocker earrings cuz' I get easily confused as a "gringa," which I hate . . . jajaja!!!

**MM:** Do you feel that there is anything in your art that has been overlooked or not recognized?

**SM:** . . . maybe the fact I was one of the first Latinas with such a big mural in Times Square?

**MM:** What excites you in contemporary art today?

**SM:** The fact that artists are not afraid to be diverse and submerge into other medias like advertising, design, fashion, music, and other fields. Breaking with the canon of "the Artist," and integrating more to society . . . similar to the Bauhaus ideals.

# INTERVIEW WITH MICKALENE THOMAS

**Matthew McLendon:** Your background and training are fairly well documented. What is something that you feel has been important to your evolution as an artist that has been overlooked?

**Mickalene Thomas:** One thing that I think may get overlooked is the broad range of ideas and imagery that influence my work. A lot gets said about the influence of this sort of nostalgic recollection of the popular imagery from the 1970s and the overt references I make to the Western canon and the "masters" of modern art. People tend to focus on the portraits and the imagery I use, but my work is actually fairly process-driven. I believe that it is imperative that I continue to develop and grow as an artist and that my work changes as well. My work has evolved organically over time, often leading me to a point I might not have imagined when I first started out with those early portraits. For example, I started out with a fairly simple process of photographing a woman or scene and then making a painting. Over time, this process has grown to include the creation of collages, independent installations, and videos. As I expand the scope of the work, my touchstone is always the piece at hand, its relationship to the rest of my work, the broader canon, and how it functions formally. I often say that I consider myself an abstract painter. This process has led me quite naturally to landscape and still life painting, as well as video work, arriving at what might seem to be surprising subject matter by following a conceptual thread discovered through the studio process.

**MM:** As you've just said, your work displays an overt and deep knowledge of the Western canon and you have cited artists such as Manet and Matisse as influences. Why do you feel it is important for your work to enter into this dialogue with the past?

**MT:** History is important whether it's art history, political history, or cultural history—it allows you to gain an understanding of the language that has developed and where you might contribute to the discussion or dispute what has come before. Of course, I could choose to enter into the discussion at any historical point, but art from the late nineteenth and early twentieth century is of particular interest to me both because I see it as the root of the formal discussions still happening in art today and also because it really marks the time when female models started to assert their own identity and presence through the gaze. Around this time, at least in the contemporary discourse, the sitters for the classic genre nude cease to be anonymous props and begin to insist on their individuality with their gaze. Because I began my work as a way of representing figures largely absent in the canon—African American women—I feel a kinship and imperative to interact with these pivotal figurative painters. As my work has developed, I return to the past as a way of determining what is missing, what I can add, to the conversations in painting I find most interesting.

**MM:** Your process includes the construction of elaborate sets or backdrops as well as photo shoots, which have been likened to editorial fashion shoots. The process, therefore, seems grounded in theatricality or, even, a type of performance. Do you agree with this assessment?

**MT:** I started out by photographing myself and using photography as a way of drawing or sketching my ideas for a painting. To this end, I would aim to make the photographs as compositionally compelling as I wanted the paintings. Inevitably, this led to more and more complex installations and photo staging. I soon realized that this was a body of work in its own right—I was creating

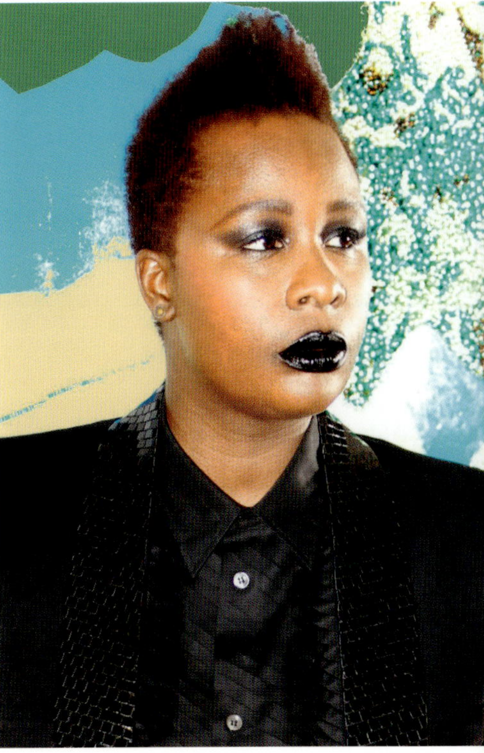

Courtesy of the artist and Lehmann Maupin Gallery, New York

highly specific tableaus similar to those created in the early days of photography when photographers were still taking their cues from painting.

From the beginning, my work has been grounded in performance. Some of my earliest portraits are of myself in the character of Quanikah (such as the photograph, *Quanikah Goes Up*, 2002), a sort of alter-ego that I would embody during my time at Yale. I developed Quanikah as a way to perform an aspect of my character and history that people don't necessarily see in my day-to-day interactions. Similarly, when I photograph the women for my work, we are creating an atmosphere, often of seduction, that allows them to play out an aspect of themselves usually reserved for private moments.

**MM:** The exhibition, *Beyond Bling: Voices of Hip-Hop in Art*, began its genesis after a viewing of your work on display at Art Basel Miami in 2007. Do you feel your art is influenced by the broad cultural phenomenon described as hip-hop?

**MT:** It is always surprising to me when people draw a connection between my work and hip-hop, but I am certainly pleased that my work would help inspire an exhibition! I don't necessarily think my work is directly inspired by hip-hop, though I would say that I believe hip-hop has helped to shape the broader cultural landscape that informs my work. I see this especially in the way sampling and mixing have developed as strategies for representing more than one view/cultural reference at a time and the way in which hip-hop has been instrumental in asserting that there are multiple levels of interpretation available in any given artistic expression. I believe that my work and hip-hop have developed from similar artistic impulses and employ some of the same conceptual strategies. If you think back to the earliest days of hip-hop with its heavy use of sampling to quote and reshape what had musically come before in order to assert a new musical and cultural identity, that is almost exactly what I am doing with my work. I look back through the canon of Western art, quote what I feel is especially relevant to my experience as an African American woman now or, conversely, insert figures that I can identify with into a period or genre where they have been historically lacking. Aesthetically, there is an element of artifice and certainly baroque decorative tendencies present in both my work and the performative aspects of hip-hop though in my work I am using decorative elements not as an assertion of wealth and power, but as a formal strategy that carries an allusion to artifice, performance, and non-traditional media. I can also identify with the urge to express a vision in the most pure, sincere form possible; I make my work from a place of sincere desire for self-expression, and I think the best hip-hop artists do the same.

**MM:** Can you explain a bit more about these "baroque decorative tendencies" and the relationship between these rather glamorous surfaces of enamel, rhinestones, and sequins and the subject matter of your work?

**MT:** One of the main themes in my work concerns the idea of self-presentation and representation. In portraiture, you are always dealing with the surface—the presentation of the sitter. As the artist, I use surface-level clues as indicators of what lies beneath the surface of the individual. With my portraits, I seek to capture and translate a moment that occurs while photographing the model that is the exact moment when I sense her satisfaction of taking on a role and representing some aspect of her character through that role. Because this moment occurs during a photo shoot, while the woman is in costume and heavy make-up, there is an element of artifice and performance at play. I seek to emphasize or lay bare this aspect of the image both in the photograph where I never re-touch or Photoshop, and in the painting with my use of rhinestones and enamel. Gradually, however, the rhinestones have become another of the tools I employ to create a compelling image. My use of them originated in a very specific way but has now expanded to encompass formal concerns of texture and color as I create any of my paintings; portraits, still lifes, or landscapes. I think part of my insistence on the surface, part of the "fetishization" stems from my awareness that I am creating art objects, not just images and representations of women and landscapes. I am aware that the work I create needs to be compelling on a lot of different levels.

**MM:** Your work has, up until now, been predominately portraiture of African American women. Given your conversations with the canonical "masters" of modernism, do your surfaces further the fetishization of black skin which is a major discourse within modernist studies?

**MT:** The women in my work throw up a pretty formidable barrier to the tradition of fetishization of black skin; they look right back at the viewer with self-knowledge, demanding to be seen while creating the impression of seeing right through the viewer. In as much as I am presenting them in a way that is filled with beauty, artifice, and decoration, there is an element of fetishization. However, I think it is important to note that this presentation is one that is willful and presents an aspect of these women that they want to bring to the fore, their own particular beauty and sexual appeal as represented and embodied by themselves. The women are mesmerizing and beautiful, but they are not romanticized or ascribed any sort of power other than what they claim themselves and throw right back at the viewer.

**MM:** Do you foresee a time when you might do portraiture of Caucasian women or even men? How do you think such a change would be perceived?

**MT:** I can't possibly know how that change would be perceived by others, and as an artist, quite honestly, I can't afford to let such considerations shape my artistic decisions. This is not to say that I don't consider the viewer; I want to be effective in my communication and expression, but I can't be concerned with or try to guess at what an audience wants or expects from me. But to the first part of the question, I have done some paintings of Caucasian women, and, thus far, they have been commissions. However, as my work continues to evolve and my interests shift I see no reason that my portraiture would not eventually include white women or even men. In fact, I have one painting in mind right now that is of a white woman. . . .

**MM:** You seem to be exploring identity much of the time in your art. How do you think your work reflects the identity of African-American women in contemporary society?

**MT:** I guess when it comes to identity, I feel my art is an extension of myself. I am making my work as a personal journey and a way of placing and navigating the world that I grew up in. I think it is imperative to note that this exploration is of my, very particular experience and in an effort to represent and shape my own, very particular identity. This is a pursuit that is bound to speak to other African American women, people in general as well as myself, but certainly not to all African American women. I don't, by any means, think that I am representing a broad, defining characterization of the identity of African American women in contemporary society.

Periodically, I focus on a group of women or a particularly powerful figure in the public eye (for example, Condoleezza Rice and Oprah in *When Ends Meet*, 2007 and Michelle Obama in *Michelle O*, 2009). These portraits are a way for me to represent women that I either identify with or feel have been overlooked or misrepresented by the mainstream media. Too often, I feel that the identity of African American women in contemporary society is overly simplified or overlooked all together. My vision is of individual, complex women that have characteristics that are common to all people.

**MM:** Much of your work has a very 1970s look to it, yet it is obviously contemporary. How did you arrive at this?

**MT:** I was born in 1971, so my earliest images of women were strongly influenced by the aesthetic of that period. When I started to make portraits of women, especially when I began to paint and photograph my mother, it seemed like the natural and logical choice to style them in the manner of these formative images. My work has always come from a sincere place of self-exploration and part of the excitement of making this work has been to see how other women relate to the images I remember from my childhood. Over time, I have held onto some aspects of the 1970s aesthetic more than others; patterns, wood paneling, and costuming remain as key elements that I use with both formal and conceptual intentions.

**MM:** Yes, pattern is an important component of your compositions. Such reliance on pattern can be linked to the likes of Henri Matisse and Paul Gauguin as well as feminist art of the 1970s and 1980s. What do you see as the influences that bring this into your style?

**MT:** These influences (Matisse and Gauguin, feminist art), the general aesthetic of the 1970s, as well as the work of the African portrait photographers, Malick Sidibé and Seydou Keïta, all figure in my use of pattern. I particularly like the way that pattern can function on so many conceptual, referential levels while serving as a terrifically strong tool of color and rhythm within a given composition.

**MM:** In recent work you are focusing on landscape and still life. Is this a conscious shift away from the portrait or figurative art for which you are well known?

**MT:** The move toward landscape and still life evolved naturally out of my examination of portraiture. Over the last several years, I have become more interested in complicating and focusing on the formal elements within the portraits. Thinking about the way in which my portraits play off historical conventions, I began to consider other painterly conventions and genres. I had been doing a lot of traveling, photographing the landscape and I wanted to bring this into my studio practice. This is just the kind of evolution that I think is inherent to any worthwhile artistic endeavor. When I feel a major shift in my work, that's when I know that I'm really breaking new ground. Being okay with new ideas, regardless of what you might think is expected of you, is one of the best challenges of being an artist.

**MM:** What excites you in contemporary art today?

**MT:** What is so exciting to me is the wide-open nature of contemporary art today. Because the conversation has become so completely global, there is no longer this sense that there is an "inside" and "outside" to contemporary art. It is not necessary to be in New York to be relevant. This situation really forces both the artist and the viewer to be accountable to themselves. Sure, there are still institutions, writers, gallerists that validate some artists over others but it is no longer enough to just listen to them. Because of the wide-open nature of contemporary art, a single confirmation or dismissal of an artist's work is not enough. There are multiple ways of being relevant and contemporary, and it is up to the artist and the viewer to engage.

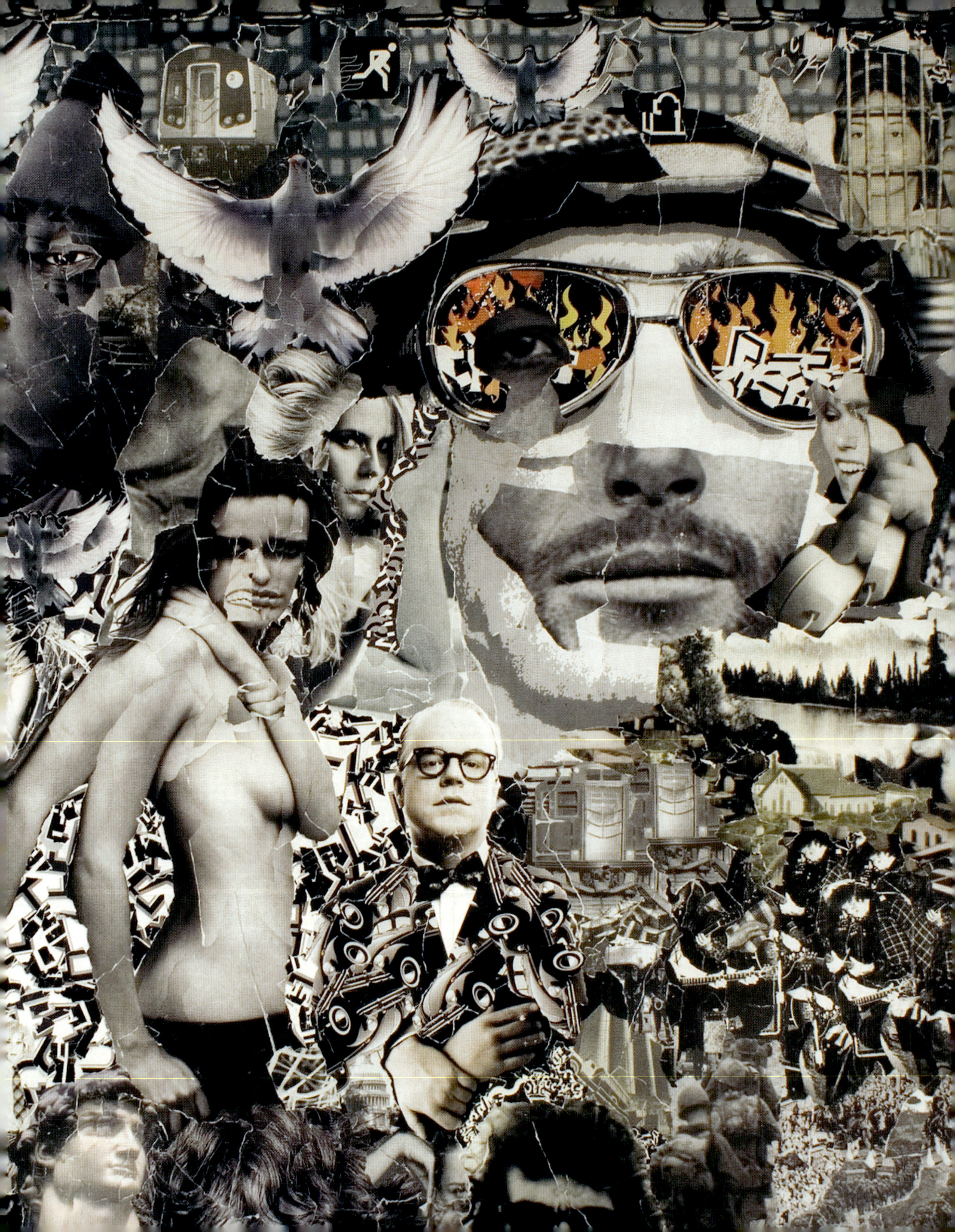

First published in 2011 by

Scala Publishers Ltd
Northburgh House
10 Northburgh Street
London EC1V 0AT, UK
www.scalapublishers.com

In association with The John and Mable Ringling Museum of Art
www.ringling.org

ISBN 978-1-85759-697-7

Project editor: Stephanie Emerson
Design: Miko McGinty, Inc.
Printed in China

10 9 8 7 6 5 4 3 2 1



Front cover: Kehinde Wiley, *Simon George I*, 2006
Frontispiece: Sofia Maldonado, 42nd Street mural, 2010 (detail)
Page 118: Michael Anderson, *Black Music vs. Helvetica*, 2009 (detail)
Back cover: Mickalene Thomas, *Ain't I a Woman (Sandra)*, 2009 (detail)